Comptroller's Handbook

A-AL

I0439149

Safety and Soundness

| Capital Adequacy (C) | Asset Quality (A) | Management (M) | Earnings (E) | Liquidity (L) | Sensitivity to Market Risk (S) | Other Activities (O) |

Agricultural Lending

May 2014

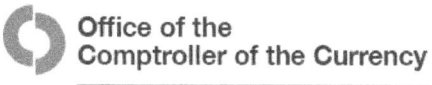

Office of the
Comptroller of the Currency

Washington, DC 20219

Contents

Introduction

The Office of the Comptroller of the Currency's (OCC) *Comptroller's Handbook* booklet, "Agricultural Lending," provides guidance for bank examiners and bankers on the risks presented by agricultural (Ag) lending activities. The booklet, one of several specialized lending booklets in the *Comptroller's Handbook*, supplements guidance contained in the "Loan Portfolio Management," "Large Bank Supervision," and "Community Bank Supervision" booklets.

The booklet discusses the general risks inherent in Ag lending and describes supervisory expectations and regulatory requirements for prudent risk management of this lending activity. It includes expanded examination procedures to guide examiners in evaluating the effect of Ag lending activities on the risk profile and financial condition of a bank. Throughout this booklet, national banks and federal savings associations are referred to collectively as banks, except when it is necessary to distinguish between the two. The glossary in appendix E contains definitions of terms used in the booklet or the Ag industry.

Overview

Ag lending is a critical business line for many banks, especially those in rural areas. Bank credit has played an important role in farm activities throughout U.S. history. Most farms in the United States remain family-owned. Financing supplied by banks is essential to many individual farm operators and to the development of new Ag technologies and techniques. As with all forms of lending, Ag credit presents the banker with a unique set of risks.

Each region of the country has unique conditions reflected in the variety of commodities produced and marketed. Typically, there is at least some Ag product diversification within a region; because of the interrelationships between many farm products and activities, and their influence on surrounding communities, however, Ag concentrations represent a key risk for many community banks. Moreover, each Ag enterprise presents unique technologies, restrictions, and challenges for both the borrower and the bank lender.

The traditional role of bank credit in the Ag industry has involved funding seasonal production and longer-term investments in land, buildings, equipment, and breeding stock. Loan repayment depends primarily on the successful production and marketing of Ag products, and secondarily on loan collateral. In some cases, income generated from work performed outside the Ag industry (nonfarm income) or work performed for other farms (off-farm income) may be available. Such income is often devoted to family living expenses, however, and may only supplement the borrower's repayment ability.

Ag lending can be a significant source of bank income but also can be the source of significant losses. While a bank cannot control commodity prices or production levels, many banks have demonstrated that diligent adherence to prudent lending practices and regulatory guidance helps manage losses, even when a borrower's farm operation experiences significant stress.

Business Description

Ag products vary widely. Different types of Ag production involve different markets, growing cycles, exposure to climate and growing conditions (including weather), perils (including fire, flood, infestations, and predation), and infrastructure costs. Depending on the type of Ag product, banks use different techniques to underwrite and administer Ag loans.

Major segments of the Ag industry include crop production, Ag real estate, Ag equipment, livestock production (such as cow-calf and feedlots), dairy, meatpacking, transportation and storage, fertilizer production and distribution, ethanol production, and seed production. Banks provide financing for a broad spectrum of Ag products, including grains (such as corn, wheat, soybeans, and rice), wine, cotton, dairy, poultry, beef, swine, nuts, fruits, and timber. In addition to the variety of products, markets, cycles, and risks that affect farm and ranch operations, local, state, and federal programs and restrictions can affect the borrower's repayment capacity.

This booklet provides an overview of fundamental principles that apply to most Ag banks and borrowers. The OCC expects bank management to have appropriate knowledge of the key risk factors relating to the types of Ag lending specific to the bank. Banks should have appropriate and reliable risk management systems in place to effectively govern Ag lending.

Agricultural Lending Markets

Repayment of Ag loans depends primarily on the successful planting and harvest of crops (or the raising and feeding of livestock) and marketing the harvested commodity (including grain, milk, hay, cattle, swine, and poultry). Typically, any illiquid collateral securing the Ag loan represents the secondary, rather than the primary, source of repayment. Similarly, loans for Ag real estate that is farmed by tenants are dependent on cash flow from tenant rental income as the primary source of repayment.

Technological advances have had a dramatic effect on Ag production. As new technologies involving fertilization, equipment, irrigation, genetics, and biotechnology have advanced, the supply of most Ag commodities has increased. These technological advances have affected virtually all sectors of the Ag industry. In many cases, larger farm operations benefit from economies of scale so they can produce products at a lower per unit cost. Larger farms, however, tend to retain more financial leverage and thus more risk.

Changes in consumers' preferences have increased demand for farm products raised in a noncommercial setting, creating niche markets often filled by smaller, independent operators. Examples of growth in niche markets include demand for organic foods, specialty crops, free-range livestock and poultry, and gluten-free products. Also, demand for certain food types can vary because of demographic changes and general public perception. Prices may rise or fall based on these changes. Examples include the mad cow disease and avian flu concerns in the early 2000s, a long-term decline in pork product demand, and a spike in egg demand related to the popularity of high protein/low carbohydrate diets.

The prices of other commodities indirectly influence Ag markets. For example, energy prices affect many farmers, because natural gas is a basic component of most inorganic nitrogen fertilizers, and gasoline and diesel fuel are used for farm equipment and transportation to market.

Banks are competitive in the Ag credit market, but nonbank lenders are increasingly competitive for certain types of Ag loans. These nonbank lenders include the following.

- **Farm Credit System (FCS):** The FCS comprises cooperative institutions regulated by the Farm Credit Administration. FCS institutions lend money to farmers through local FCS associations. Wholesale lending (to FCS institutions) is shared between the Farm Credit System Funding Corporation and the regional farm credit banks. The FCS relies exclusively on selling farm credit bonds to fund lending operations. The liability for FCS bond underwriting is jointly and severally shared by the farm credit banks and is guaranteed by the Farm Credit System Insurance Corporation. Primarily, financial institutions purchase the bonds. FCS lenders traditionally are most competitive in the Ag real estate market, because they can issue long-term bonds to offset their interest rate exposure on long-term mortgages. Other products include operating loans, intermediate-term debt for capital purchases, rural home mortgage loans, leases, credit-related life insurance, crop insurance, commercial real estate loans, and accounting/income tax preparation.
- **Farm Service Agency (FSA):** The FSA, formerly known as the Farmers Home Administration (FmHA), is the agency within the U.S. Department of Agriculture (USDA) that administers federal Ag lending programs. (Appendix C contains descriptions of the federal loan and guarantee programs.) FSA loans are funded from the USDA's budget and from funds repaid by borrowers. The FSA focuses resources on serving small, less experienced, and disadvantaged farmers.
- **Life insurance companies:** These companies primarily provide farm real estate financing to larger Ag enterprises, generally borrowers financing amounts greater than $1 million.
- **Captive lenders:** Vendors such as equipment manufacturers, seed companies, and retailers normally provide limited-purpose vendor financing to enhance market penetration for their products.
- **Other lenders:** These include parents financing their children's Ag operations, property owners providing self-financing for their tenant farmers, and individuals financing the sale of land and other capital assets using a contract for deed or sales contract.

Authority and Limits

National banks and federal savings associations are permitted by statute to engage in Ag lending. The authority for national banks is found in 12 USC 24, while the authority for federal savings associations is found in 12 USC 1464.

No exposure limit applies regarding a national bank's Ag lending activities, provided that the volume and nature of the Ag lending does not pose unwarranted risk to the bank's financial condition.

Certain exposure limitations apply to federal savings associations, as set forth in 12 USC 1464(c) and 12 CFR 160.30. Ag loans typically are classified as commercial loans, which cannot exceed 20 percent of total assets, provided that amounts in excess of 10 percent of assets are small business loans.[1] A federal savings association may make Ag loans under other authority, however, depending on the circumstances.[2] For example, to the extent nonresidential real property secures an Ag loan, a federal savings association may make the loan under its nonresidential real property loan authority.[3]

Risks Associated With Agricultural Lending

From a supervisory perspective, risk is the potential that events, expected or unexpected, will have an adverse effect on a bank's earnings, capital, or franchise or enterprise value. The OCC has defined eight categories of risk for bank supervision purposes: credit, interest rate, liquidity, price, operational, compliance, strategic, and reputation. These categories are not mutually exclusive. Any product or service may expose a bank to multiple risks. Risks also may be interdependent and may be positively or negatively correlated. Examiners should be aware of this interdependence and assess the effect in a consistent and inclusive manner. Refer to the "Bank Supervision Process" booklet of the *Comptroller's Handbook* for an expanded discussion of banking risks and their definitions.

The risks associated with Ag lending are credit, interest rate, liquidity, operational, compliance, strategic, and reputation.

Credit Risk

Banks must assess the level of Ag-related credit risk and the adequacy of bank capital to withstand potential future market and economic distress. Banks financing Ag operations and capital investment assume risk associated with the borrower's ability to successfully plant crops or breed animals, grow or raise the product, harvest finished products (such as grains and livestock for slaughter) or partially finished products (such as feeder cattle and raw cotton), and deliver products to market. In reviewing a bank's Ag credit risk, it is critical to remember that market conditions are often volatile. Prolonged adverse Ag market conditions can increase borrower defaults and significantly impair collateral value, negatively affecting a bank's ability to withstand a sustained market downturn.

---

[1] 12 USC 1464(c)(2)(A): Small business loans include any loan to a small business (defined in 12 CFR 160.3 and 13 CFR 121) and any loan that does not exceed $2 million and is for commercial, corporate, business, or agricultural purposes. See the definitions of "Small Business Loans and Loans to Small Businesses" and "Small Business" in 12 CFR 160.3.

[2] 12 CFR 160.31(a) provides that if a loan is authorized under more than one section of the Home Owners' Loan Act, a federal savings association may designate under which section the loan has been made. Such a loan may be apportioned among appropriate categories.

[3] 12 USC 1464(c)(2)(B) generally limits nonresidential real property loans to 400 percent of the federal savings association's capital.

Ag borrowers' repayment capacities are vulnerable to risks including adverse weather conditions, commodity price volatility, diseases, land values, production costs, changing government regulations and subsidy programs, changing tax treatment, technological changes, labor market shortages, and changes in consumers' preferences. Many of these risks may not be under the borrower's control; borrowers, however, can use risk management plans to mitigate many of these risks. This includes use of diversification strategies (crop or product mix), purchased insurance, operations integration, hedging, or contracting strategies.

Production Risk

Banks financing crops or livestock assume the risk associated with the borrower's ability to successfully raise and market the commodity. Adverse weather conditions and other natural perils can dramatically affect farmers' or ranchers' production and ability to service debt. Grain farmers can mitigate the risk of losses from natural disasters by obtaining crop insurance, and farmers and ranchers can make capital improvements to their land to prevent soil erosion and flooding. Farmers may spray their crops with pesticides to prevent insect infestations, and ranchers often vaccinate their livestock to prevent diseases.

Production problems may also cause unbudgeted expenses that reduce profitability or even result in losses. Unexpected expenses may occur because of increased production or harvesting costs caused by inclement weather, higher transportation or fertilization costs caused by market disruption, feed shortages, etc. Business cycles longer than one year (e.g., vineyards, orchards, and some livestock operations) may increase the risk of unexpected expenses.

Market Volatility

Volatile commodity prices present another significant risk for Ag borrowers and Ag lenders. Large price fluctuations can occur because of unfavorable weather, domestic and global supply and demand changes, and macro changes in political or economic policy. Market price volatility and production cost volatility can affect both revenues (output) and expenses (input). Because many Ag products are globally traded commodities, currency exchange rate volatility may also affect prices. Some Ag products are marketed locally, such as vegetables, while other products are primarily marketed on a national basis or are simply more competitive domestically due to tariffs, growing conditions, or other influences. Rapid rises in interest rates can cause increased capitalization rates, resulting in reduced farmland values. All of these factors can present risk to an Ag borrower's repayment capacity.

Farmers and ranchers can mitigate market risk by using a variety of strategies. These include diversifying crop and livestock products, hedging commodities under production, contracting (pre-selling) production, and hedging or contracting input commodities. Accurate budgeting and financial management play crucial roles in whether such strategies are successful. The bank must have a sound understanding of the financial effect these strategies have on Ag borrowers.

Government Policies and Legal Risks

Changes in government policies can have dramatic effects on Ag producers. Regulations may differ between states or even local jurisdictions. Some segments of the Ag industry can potentially cause significant pollution, soil damage, or erosion. There are extensive state and federal regulations pertaining to access and environmental remediation that apply to many Ag operators. Additionally, government restrictions can affect the type of Ag operations that are permissible in certain areas. For example, large swine, dairy, cattle feedlot, and poultry operations generate significant animal waste. These large Ag operations are often not permitted to operate near significant population centers. In addition, nutrient management plans are typically needed to limit the amount of animal waste applied to cropland on an annual basis. Some Ag producers also face legal and reputation risks from accidents involving potential environmental contamination or health concerns, such as E. coli outbreaks associated with certain foods.

Government Ag assistance policies are also affected by periodic reforms in legislation. Depending on the degree of reliance on government assistance, these changes can have varying impact on a borrower's repayment capacity. For example, the Agricultural Act of 2014 ("Farm Bill") eliminated direct payments to Ag producers while continuing crop insurance options, rural development programs, and conservation programs. Further, the Farm Bill eliminated some tax subsidies for corn ethanol producers.

Limited Purpose Collateral

The limited purpose of some Ag-related collateral affects credit risk because such collateral may have limited or no other uses to support values when loan repayment problems emerge. For example, a broiler barn may have little residual value if a poultry grower loses a processing contract. Additionally, commodity prices and land values are highly correlated, especially in Ag regions where farmland has no other use. Conversely, regions with multiple uses for land may have minimal correlation between land values and commodity prices.

Interest Rate Risk

Most Ag operating lines that banks finance are either short-term or variable rate loans, resulting in lower interest rate risk. A bank that provides fixed-rate financing for extended terms (on farmland, for example) exposes itself to interest rate risk to the extent that shorter-term liabilities fund these longer-term loans. To mitigate interest rate risk in financing real estate, banks may underwrite these longer-term loans with a three- to five-year balloon payment to provide the opportunity for repricing the loans at maturity. Additionally, the bank may have increased credit risk exposure in a rising rate environment as Ag borrower's repayment ability is reduced by higher borrowing costs.

Liquidity Risk

Ag lending can result in higher liquidity risk for banks, especially banks with large Ag credit concentrations. For example, if crop losses or unfavorable market conditions result in loan payment deferrals, the bank's liquidity could be strained. In addition, discontinued farm operations and migration to urban areas can cause declining deposits, creating longer-term liquidity pressure at some banks.

Operational Risk

Operational risk primarily results from the extensive documentation, inspection, control, and monitoring requirements associated with Ag lending. Failure to comply with such requirements can lead to loan collection problems. In addition, improper controls can unnecessarily expose the bank to losses and increased operational risk, particularly if loan collateral is sold out of trust.

Failing to properly document a loan supported by a government guarantee can result in the bank's inability to collect on the guarantee if needed. This is most often the result of lender complacence or inappropriate assumptions about a borrower or collateral. Further, lien perfection requirements for Ag collateral can vary depending on property type and legal requirements in different areas. If liens are not properly perfected, banks may not be protected by collateral when liquidation, repossession, or foreclosure becomes necessary. Evidence of collateral lien perfection and timely collateral inspections should be documented in the loan file.

Compliance Risk

Compared with consumer transactions, there are few borrower-focused rules regulating Ag financing. Ag lending is subject to Equal Credit Opportunity Act (Regulation B) (12 CFR 1002) nondiscrimination requirements, however, and may be subject to zoning, environmental protection, and other government regulations if real estate serves as collateral. Failure to ensure compliance with these requirements can expose the bank to liability and jeopardize ultimate repayment. Failure to comply with Regulation B may result in supervisory actions. There are also banking regulations that govern the bank's management of risk. These include

- "Lending Limits," 12 CFR 32 (national banks and federal savings associations). (See appendix D.)
- "Appraisals," 12 CFR 34, subpart C (national banks), and 12 CFR 164 (federal savings associations). (See the "Collateral Valuation" section of this booklet.)
- "Real Estate Lending Standards," 12 CFR 34, subpart D (national banks), and 12 CFR 160.101 (federal savings associations). (See the "Loan Policy and Governance" section of this booklet.)
- "Loans in Areas Having Special Flood Hazards," 12 CFR 22 (national banks) and 12 CFR 172 (federal savings associations). (See the "Collateral Documentation" section of this booklet.)

Failure to comply with these regulations can result in supervisory actions or significant losses.

Strategic Risk

A sound Ag lending program requires management to ensure that the staff has the knowledge and experience to recognize, assess, mitigate, and monitor the bank's unique Ag risks. Prudent Ag lending requires specialized expertise. Failure to provide effective oversight of Ag activities can increase the bank's strategic risk profile while also negatively affecting interrelated risks, such as credit and reputation risks.

Reputation Risk

Banks with lending activities to borrowers in certain Ag enterprises can face increased reputation risk. For example, a bank may finance operations generating large amounts of animal waste that could potentially contaminate water sources or cause other ecosystem damage. Public perception and potential litigation may cast the bank, along with the borrower, as an adversary to be held responsible for environmental cleanup. Costs relating to remediation of environmental contamination and potential liabilities may exceed the amount of the original loan.

In addition, the bank can damage its reputation if it reduces the availability of farm credit or forecloses on farm collateral. Many Ag lenders do business in small, rural communities. Constructively working with borrowers often benefits the bank and the borrower. Lending decisions that are not publicly perceived as favorable to the community may have a significant effect on the bank's Ag lending activities. For example, if the bank forecloses on a family farm owned for generations, the community may negatively view the bank's foreclosure action even if the action was a prudent business decision.

Risk Management

The OCC expects each bank to identify, measure, monitor, and control risk by implementing an effective risk management system appropriate for its size and the complexity of its operations. When examiners assess the effectiveness of a bank's risk management system, they consider the bank's policies, processes, personnel, and control systems. Refer to the "Bank Supervision Process" and "Loan Portfolio Management" booklets of the *Comptroller's Handbook* for expanded discussions of risk management.

Loan Policy and Governance

A bank's loan policy should address Ag lending objectives and risk appetite, including acceptable types of Ag loans, portfolio distribution, lending market or territory, and risk limits expressed as a percentage of the bank's capital. The policy should establish requirements for the structure, reporting lines, and oversight of the Ag lending department or program. The Ag lending policy should also establish prudent underwriting standards and approval requirements specific to the type of the bank's lending activities. Consideration should be given to financial analysis expectations, advance rates on various types of crops or livestock, pricing parameters, loan covenants, and structure expectations. Additionally, policies should address Ag credit administration and loan documentation standards pertinent to the scope and type(s) of Ag lending, including

- financial documentation and repayment capacity analysis, including updates on outside debt.
- budget or cash flow projection analysis.
- liquidity monitoring.
- stress testing.
- guarantor analysis, when applicable.
- crop and livestock inspection requirements, including appropriate frequency and timing of inspections and valuations.
- equipment inspections and valuation expectations.
- expectations for the content and frequency of real estate evaluations and appraisals.
- title and lien verification.
- insurance policy requirements.
- frequency of credit checks.

A bank's policies and procedures should address risks posed by individual loans as well as aggregate Ag portfolio risk. Even when individual Ag loans are prudently underwritten, groups of loans that are similarly affected by internal and external market factors may expose the bank to a heightened level of risk and warrant increased board and management attention. The OCC expects banks with significant credit risk concentrations, including concentrations in Ag-related loans, to maintain appropriate capital levels to mitigate the concentration risk. There also may be cases in which the potential risk to capital is so severe that reduction of the concentration or suspension of Ag loan originations is the most effective risk mitigation action.

The lending policy should address expectations for appropriately mitigating loan policy exceptions. The policy should address the bank's approval process required for each type or size of lending transaction, as well as requirements for reporting exceptions to the board or a designated committee of the board. The policy should also require management to review data on an individual and aggregate basis. Aggregated data can provide a more complete picture of credit risk in the portfolio and reveal potential vulnerability in the underwriting process or in the policy itself.

The board is responsible for ensuring control systems are implemented to monitor compliance with established Ag lending policies. The level of compliance should be incorporated into the bank's allowance for loan and lease losses (ALLL) analysis, capital and liquidity planning processes, and the board's strategic-planning efforts. The bank's Ag lending policies should be updated as needed. Additionally, the bank's Ag lending policies should be reviewed and approved by the board annually.

Bank management should also provide the board an analysis of the risk posed by Ag lending activities, as well as risks correlated to the Ag industry and their potential effects on the bank's asset quality, earnings, capital, and liquidity.

Staffing

The board, management, and Ag lending staff should possess sufficient technical expertise corresponding to the volume and complexity of the bank's Ag portfolio. Given the general decline in farm and rural populations, some Ag-focused community banks have had difficulty developing and retaining qualified staff for key positions. As a result, board planning for staff retention and management succession is critical. The board should ensure that the bank's Ag loan officers are sufficient in number to grant and administer credits in accordance with the bank's policy. The depth of experience and expertise within the Ag lending department or function should enable continuity during times of change or adversity. Additionally, sufficient resources should be allocated to Ag staff development and continuing education.

Underwriting

Prudent Ag loan underwriting shares many of the same characteristics as commercial lending in other industries, including strong emphasis on borrower cash flow and repayment capacity. Ag banks should not place undue reliance on collateral and cyclical factors as part of underwriting decisions. Along these lines, banks should be sensitive to evidence of speculation in Ag land prices or commodities that influence the market. For example, an Ag loan approval should be based on a reasonable expectation that operating cash flow will provide sufficient repayment, not on the Ag land value.

Comprehensive assessment of the borrower's creditworthiness and cash flow is critical. A successful Ag business should exhibit strong repayment capacity, liquidity, solvency, collateral, profitability, and management performance. Conversely, highly leveraged Ag borrowers or borrowers in a weakened financial condition are more vulnerable to rapid or extended financial distress.

Ag underwriting criteria should consider the borrower's experience and track record in managing a farming or ranching operation. Because a farmer's or rancher's cash flow is often seasonal or cyclical, appropriate loan structure is critical to managing credit risk within an Ag lending relationship. Banks must thoroughly understand the Ag borrower's cash flow cycles and structure loans accordingly.

The underwriting process begins with current, accurate, and complete financial information, including a reliable budget or cash flow projection. Current borrower information is essential to the bank's ability to evaluate a borrower's creditworthiness and leverage. Current credit information generally is considered to be no more than 12 months old. The bank's loan policy should detail specific requirements for credit information and analysis.

Effective written guidelines should govern the underwriting process and subsequent loan administration. At a minimum, the guidelines should require the following:

- Thorough evaluation of the borrower's farming or ranching experience and historical performance managing debt obligations.

- In-depth financial analysis of the borrower and any guarantors. This may include analysis of financial statements, income tax returns, cash flow, interim financial statements for large farms such as livestock operations, or recent credit bureau reports.
- Evaluation of budgets and projections for yield, weight gain, production costs, and commodity prices. This includes stress testing the budget, developing an understanding of critical assumptions, and evaluating the degree of reasonableness and reliability. Comparison of prior budgets and financial projections with current budgets and actual results should be part of this process.
- A sensitivity analysis that determines a farm or ranch operation's ability to withstand risk and uncertainty as part of cash flow projection analysis.
- Structuring loans in accordance with the type of Ag borrowing and the expected source of repayment.
- Maximum advance rates for each type of Ag product.
- Minimum standards for borrower debt service, net worth, liquidity, and leverage.
- Maximum loan term, minimum amortization, and pricing expectations.
- Timely and reliable collateral valuations, including current crop and livestock inspections, reliable and well-supported equipment valuations, and independent real estate evaluations or appraisals that comply with regulatory requirements.
- Effective financial and reporting covenants, based on the size and complexity of the farm operation.
- Criteria addressing the borrower's risk management plans, including risk-mitigating tools for insuring crop production and marketing commodities produced by the farm.

Once this information is understood, lenders are equipped to effectively structure the lending relationship.

Loan Structure

At a minimum, lenders should structure loans based on the nature of the borrower's Ag business and the loan purpose. A key consideration for structuring Ag loans is to understand the farmer's or rancher's operations and the timing of revenue and expenses. Proper loan structure requires support by sufficient cash flow from the expected source of repayment. Borrower challenges and problems should be anticipated and included in the loan structure.

The bank should match the loan type and terms to the loan purpose and likely sources of repayment. The bank should develop appropriate terms, amortization requirements, pricing structure, financial reporting requirements, collateral value, and financial covenants to protect the bank for the term of the loan. Proper structuring of farm or ranch relationships involves securing the credit facility with collateral. Loan structure should also consider the need for additional loan support, including loan guarantees provided by financially responsible parties.

Short-term loans: Most loans to finance crop and livestock production are self-liquidating from the sale of grain or livestock produced during the operating cycle. The production (or growing) cycle should govern the maximum amount of revolving Ag credit available at any one time. An operating line of credit is generally secured by the growing crop or livestock.

The anticipated value of production determines the loan amount and dictates the availability of funds.

Typically, a borrower can draw against the line as many times and as often as needed up to a predetermined amount for given stages of development. As a general rule, all anticipated costs required to take a crop from planting to harvest are included in a farmer's short-term operating line. These "input" costs include fuel, labor, fertilizer, seed, land rent, and any other operating costs associated with the production cycle. Unanticipated costs may require additional short-term credit to ensure production; for example, poor seed emergence resulting from excessive rainfall can require replanting. In such circumstances, the borrower comes under increased pressure to generate sufficient cash flow to cover the higher operating costs and repay the operating line. Alternatively, the borrower may purposely carry short-term production credit beyond the current growing cycle to store grain or defer sales in anticipation of higher market prices.

For crop and livestock operations with short production cycles, such as grains or feeder cattle, the loans may be structured to be annually repaid and renewed. For crops involving long growing cycles, such as timber or aquaculture, a level of principal amortization is generally required well before maturity. The outstanding balance of the loan should fluctuate with the cash needs of the borrower, subject to the availability constraints of established financial covenants or other controls within the loan agreement.

Medium-term loans: Medium-term operating loans may be up to three years in length and typically involve secured real estate as additional collateral. When financing operating loans with longer-term structures, it is prudent that the bank obtains updated financial information annually and resets the loan terms based on an updated risk analysis.

Long-term loans: More commonly referred to as term loans, this type of debt is normally associated with the purchase or development of capital assets, such as real estate, machinery and equipment, breeding herds, and orchards. Final maturities vary, depending on the useful life of the asset or collateral pledged. Breeding livestock (cattle) are normally amortized over three years, machinery and equipment over five to seven years, and real estate up to 30 years. The primary source of repayment normally is cash flow from operations, with liquidation of collateral viewed only as a contingent, secondary source.

Carryover debt: Carryover debt refers to the portion of an Ag operating line that the borrower cannot repay from operating production revenue (for example, from crop, livestock, or milk sales). It represents a substitute for investment capital and must be serviced through future cash flow, sale of unencumbered assets, or other sources. The presence of significant carryover debt may require restructuring the borrower's overall debt exposure. Depending on variables including the borrower's leverage position, projected cash flows, and balance sheet, it may be appropriate to restructure carryover debt into amortizing medium-term loans while continuing to finance current operations with short-term loans. See the "Risk Rating" section of this booklet for more information on carryover debt.

Financial Analysis

Prudent Ag loan underwriting requires lenders to have a thorough understanding of the borrower's operating environment and cash flow. Because an Ag borrower's cash flow is vulnerable to a wide range of risks, lenders should have a complete understanding of the borrower's cash flow sensitivity and balance sheet. It is important for Ag lenders to obtain and analyze financial information annually using consistent financial statement dates.

The quality of financial information for Ag operations varies significantly. In general, Ag borrowers file cash-based income tax returns and prepare self-prepared and unaudited estimated market value financial statements. Larger operations may submit audited, accrual-basis financial statements; farm-related income tax returns, however, are filed on a cash basis. The bank should obtain information on the borrower's and guarantor's repayment capacity and financial condition, including income, liquidity, cash flow, contingent liabilities, and other relevant factors.

A global assessment of Ag borrower cash flow and repayment ability is often appropriate and necessary. Global cash flow analyses can be complex and may often require integrating cash flows from multiple partnership and corporate tax returns, business financial statements, K-1 tax schedules, and personal tax returns. Adjustments for required and discretionary cash flows from all activities should be reflected in the bank's cash flow analysis. Lenders should develop an understanding of any actual or contingent liabilities and their potential effect on repayment capacity, including outstanding credit card debt and vendor financing.

To assess the borrower's long-term repayment capacity, the global cash flow assessment should focus on recurring cash flows. Nonrecurring capital gains should not be considered a reliable repayment source, but ongoing capital gains from the sale of breeding stock should be included in the cash flow analysis. The bank should also require realistic family living expense projections and personal debt payments, property and income taxes, and other obligations.

When reviewing a farm or ranch operation's cash flow, it is important to understand that farmers and ranchers have the option of reporting income for tax purposes on either a cash or accrual basis. As a result, reported cash flow levels may require further analysis. Banks should strive to obtain and analyze annual financial statements that correspond with the date of the borrower's income tax returns. This provides bank management with reliable information pertaining to income and cash flow. This information is needed to accurately make accrual adjustments to the Ag borrower's cash-based tax return, providing a more reliable estimate of the farmer's repayment capacity. By using cash accounting, the timing of crop sales and purchase of supplies can be used to minimize taxes. For instance, fertilizer can be bought at year-end, expensed to the preceding crop, and used in the next tax year. The purpose of this treatment is to minimize the effects of losses in bad years by allowing expenses to be allocated to good years.

Ideally, inspections and cash flow projection analyses should occur at the same approximate time each year, because the value of the assets under production changes throughout the growing cycle. For example, a grain farmer who plants in the spring would have cash needs to purchase seed and fertilizer early in the season and draw on the line of credit. At this point in the growing cycle, there would be little to no development of the grain. As a result, comparisons to previous production just before harvest, when the grain has matured, have negligible meaning. Consequently, analyses of inspections, budget or cash flow projection variance, net worth change, leverage, liquidity, and cash flow should be compared with the same periods from prior years.

Sensitivity analysis in the underwriting process should estimate the effect of sustained changes in market conditions on the farmer's or rancher's repayment ability. As part of the underwriting process, banks should prepare base case and sensitivity analyses on the borrower's cash flow and repayment ability. A base case analysis uses assumption scenarios based on current prices and average production levels. A sensitivity case analysis subjects the farmer's or rancher's production to adverse external factors such as lower production, lower market prices, higher operating expenses, or higher interest rates to ascertain the effect on loan repayment. In both the base case and the sensitivity case, projections should reflect borrowers' ability to repay debt within a reasonable period without excessively increasing leverage.

Growing crops or livestock, machinery and equipment, and real estate are all significant assets on a farmer's or rancher's balance sheet. The value of farm production is subject to price volatility and production variability. Equipment is subject to depreciation, especially if used excessively or under harsh conditions. Because farming operations are highly capital intensive, the Ag lender needs to analyze and assess the borrower's balance sheet to understand how changes in the operating environment or market conditions would affect the borrower's financial condition. Leverage position, liquidity, and access to capital are all critical to the borrower's ability to withstand adversity.

Bank management should ensure Ag lenders perform comprehensive, global cash flow analyses even in the presence of significant liquid assets, because the borrower or guarantor may need liquidity to meet other obligations. While liquid assets may be used to support repayment, bank management must ensure that the assets are verified and available to support repayment needs.

If possible, the bank should determine a guarantor's willingness to service debt and track record in honoring previous commitments. Some guarantees may be limited in nature, such as covering interest only or partial principal, and may be limited to a specific time frame or crop production cycle.

Risk Mitigation

Ag borrowers are subject to fluctuating market prices, extreme weather conditions, and other perils that can jeopardize repayment. As a result, various tools are often used to mitigate risk.

Government programs: Various government programs may limit the risk of farming. As an example, by entering cropland into the Conservation Reserve Program, farmers contractually commit to eliminate crop production on that land. The farmer receives annual payments established by bid at the inception of the contract, which typically runs five to 10 years. Additionally, when available, federal government price supports for certain crops provide commodity price risk mitigation to both the Ag borrower and the bank.

Crop insurance: Borrowers purchase crop insurance to protect themselves against either the loss of crops caused by natural disasters such as hail, drought, and floods or the loss of revenue caused by declines in prices of Ag commodities. These two general categories of crop insurance are called crop yield insurance and crop revenue insurance.

Revenue-based crop insurance policies compensate farmers for shortfalls in crop revenues relative to their baseline averages and may also allow for increased payments if harvest prices exceed planting season prices. Farmers choose the percentage of historical coverage they want, and the insurance guarantees that amount. The farmers are paid if the harvest yield or crop prices lead to revenue shortfalls. Additionally, unless farmers choose a harvest price exclusion option, their revenue protection targets increase if commodity prices at harvest exceed the pre-planting prices.

Premium costs vary depending on the specifics of the coverage. Farmers generally have the option to obtain coverage on all or part of their acreage in production. This can be done on an enterprise-wide basis or by specific piece of property.

Yield-based crop insurance policies pay farmers for a percentage of yield shortfalls relative to their average crop history or the average yields in their county. Farmers can select the percentage of yield differential they will receive. Unit prices are based on the pre-planting price per unit set in futures contracts.

Crop hail insurance is another form of yield insurance available to provide coverage against loss to growing crops caused by hail. Depending on the crop insured, a crop hail policy may also provide coverage for loss caused by fire, lightning, wind (when accompanied by hail), vandalism, or malicious mischief. The crop may also be insured while in transportation and during storage.

Banks should be able to obtain information from borrowers pertaining to whether yield or revenue insurance coverage was selected, crop pricing options, percentage of coverage, and whether the borrower is in compliance with the terms of the contract.

Forward contracting: Producers often use contracts with packers or grain buyers to market their production. These contracts vary widely and require careful analysis, because the contracts sometimes increase risks rather than mitigate them. For example, farmers or grain elevators that use substantial forward contracting in areas where yields decline while prices increase can be adversely affected in two ways. In a typical year, farmers using forward sales or futures contracts to lock in prices before harvest deliver their crops and collect a "protected" contract price. If farmers cannot deliver the amount of grain promised in the contract, they could be forced to either purchase grain at a price higher than the contract or settle the shortfall in cash. Banks should know which borrowers have executed futures or forward sales contracts, and the borrower's ability to deliver or settle on the contracts.

It is important to evaluate counterparty risk. The counterparty to a farmer's forward sales contract is often the local grain elevator. When an elevator enters into a contract to purchase grain from a farmer, the elevator usually offsets that position with a future or forward contract to sell an equivalent amount of grain. If the farmer cannot deliver the contracted amount or provide cash settlement, the elevator still has to settle its contract in the derivatives market. Banks may find that elevator operators are unable to meet their debt service due to this issue. Banks that lend to grain elevators should be able to quantify the elevators' use of derivatives and assess the resulting financial risks.

Hedging: Hedging is used to mitigate the effect of market volatility through the buying or selling of futures contracts—legally binding commitments to sell or buy a commodity in the future at a previously determined price. Futures contracts for each type of commodity have standardized, non-negotiable features, such as quantity, quality, and time and place of delivery. Only the price component of a futures contract is negotiable. Most futures contracts do not result in delivery of the physical commodity. Instead, the contract's delivery requirement is offset when the owner of a contract takes an equal and opposite position. For example, a projection of record harvests may give a farmer the incentive to sell a futures contract to lock in the price at which a farmer can sell a particular commodity at a future date. Alternatively, a farmer wishing to protect against rapid price increases in the cost of feed may purchase a contract to take future delivery at a predetermined cost. Options can be used as an alternative to purchasing futures contracts and do not contain the risk associated with margin calls. An option provides the right, but not the obligation, to buy or sell a futures contract, at a predetermined price on or before a predetermined expiration date.

Borrowing base certificates and loan covenants: Many farm lenders require protective covenants and other affirmative undertakings by the borrower as part of the loan underwriting process. Frequently, this includes establishing financial ratios and collateral margins the borrower must maintain during the term of the loan. Such arrangements may require the borrower to periodically provide the bank with a completed certificate attesting to compliance with collateral margins and other conditions—including financial covenants. The bank should review borrower-prepared compliance certificates for reasonableness and accuracy.

These controls help the bank detect trends and early signs of credit deterioration. For example, evidence of declining collateral margins may indicate emerging concerns relating to the borrower's financial capacity and can adversely affect the bank's collateral protection in the event of default. Similarly, the bank should monitor credit lines for significant variances to planned expenses. When a borrower requests an advance that significantly exceeds projected expenses, the bank should assess the purpose of the advance, evaluate the effect on the operation, and determine whether repayment capacity is compromised. This helps the bank ensure that funds are advanced only for approved purposes.

Collateral Documentation

Complete and accurate lien perfection is crucial to protect the bank's collateral interest. Ag collateral most often consists of chattel (personal property including livestock, crops, or equipment) and real estate. The methods for obtaining and perfecting security interests in each type of collateral are dictated by the Uniform Commercial Code (UCC) and the real estate laws of each state.

- **Chattel liens:** The model UCC, which provides the process for securing chattel collateral, has been adopted with minor variations in all states except Louisiana. (Louisiana's guidelines for securing chattel are primarily outlined in the state's Napoleonic guide, although certain portions of the UCC have been adopted.) Examiners should become familiar with the relevant state's securitization and perfection requirements for the type of collateral reviewed. In general, such requirements include obtaining a signed security agreement and filing appropriate documentation with either the county or state, depending on the type of collateral perfected. With some types of collateral, multiple filings may be necessary to ensure lien perfection.

  Lien searches should be completed for each loan to assure the lender of its position relative to other lenders and to identify other creditors. Lenders must also ensure UCC filings remain current; most UCC filings expire in five years and have specific renewal requirements. The bank should also be aware of state-specific laws that offer suppliers or landlords lien positions that supersede the bank's lien position.

  Attorneys, title companies, or bank personnel can perform lien searches, and all findings should be documented in the loan file. Negative findings need prompt and appropriate action and resolution.

  Section 1324 of the Food Security Act of 1985 (7 USC 1631) contains additional notification and filing provisions designed to protect purchasers of farm products from liens about which they may not be aware. Under this section, the bank may safeguard its interest by providing a pre-sale notification of its security interest in the farm products directly to the farm product purchasers. This section also permits the bank to protect its interest by registering its security interest with the secretary of the state in which the farm products were produced, if that state has established a qualified central filing system.

- **Real estate mortgages and deeds of trust:** When considering real estate as collateral, a bank should first determine whether there are any existing liens against the property. As with chattel liens, attorneys, title companies, or bank personnel may perform real estate lien searches, and all findings should be documented. Because real estate loans normally are comparatively large, the bank may require title insurance and name itself as loss payee to protect against possible undisclosed title defects. Whether insured or not, the bank should review carefully any exceptions noted in the preliminary lien search or title insurance binder. If the exceptions are serious, they require remedy before the loan closing. Unpaid taxes deserve particular attention, as they normally constitute a prior or superior lien to all others.

In some small Ag communities with relatively stable real estate ownership, banks rely on an ownership and encumbrance (O&E) report to determine outstanding liens. Typically, in-house or local attorneys prepare these reports, based on periodic reviews of county records of real estate transactions. Although this is less costly, it is also a less conclusive process than a complete real estate title search. An O&E report may be acceptable in certain instances, provided the bank clearly documents and supports its decision to use such a report.

If the real estate includes a homestead or other buildings that comprise a significant portion of the total collateral value used to underwrite the Ag loan, hazard insurance (fire, flood, wind, or hail) should be obtained, with the bank named as loss payee. The bank must also be aware of whether the provisions of the Flood Disaster Preparedness Act apply to the property, and ensure insurance is obtained accordingly. (See "Loans in Areas Having Special Flood Hazards," 12 CFR 22 for national banks and 12 CFR 172 for federal savings associations.)

As with chattel collateral, the bank must ensure that its real estate collateral documents are accurately completed, properly recorded as necessary, and maintained current.

Collateral Valuation

Bank guidelines for collateral should include procedures for determining collateral values.

The current values of all collateral should be established during the underwriting process. Thereafter, stored crops and livestock should be reevaluated on a periodic basis, with the frequency increasing during periods of price volatility. Real estate, machinery, and equipment should be reevaluated whenever market conditions or other information leads the lender to believe that the collateral's original assigned value may have significantly decreased. Independently derived values usually provide the most objectivity, but regardless of who provides them, the individual should be thoroughly knowledgeable about the type of collateral being reviewed. Among the critical pieces of information the bank should document in all collateral valuations are

- identifying details about the collateral (location, age/hours of use, and overall condition).
- fair market value estimate as of a specific date.
- source of, or basis for calculating, the value estimate.

Crop and Livestock Valuation

Liquid Ag commodities, such as harvested crops and livestock, may be transported and easily purchased or sold. While the liquid nature of this collateral gives banks and Ag borrowers the flexibility to quickly raise cash when needed, it can also cause rapid shifts in the bank's collateral position and the borrower's balance sheet structure. As a result, banks need an effective collateral valuation program to monitor and verify crop or livestock collateral coverage.

An inspection and reevaluation should be performed by a qualified person other than the lending officer responsible for the credit decision. When such a separation of duties is impossible or impractical, every effort should be made to periodically reaffirm inspection results by independent means. Methods banks have used to accomplish this include periodically rotating inspection duties among bank personnel other than the primary lending officer, using outside directors as inspectors/reappraisers, and contracting the services of an independent third party. Further, a dual inspection process can provide effective controls, when feasible. This inspection approach includes a simultaneous inspection by the servicing loan officer and another qualified inspector/reappraiser independent of loan production. As with any confirmation process, greater credibility is placed on the results of inspections that are conducted unannounced.

Short-term production loans require varying degrees of collateral monitoring, in addition to financial analysis and initial collateral perfection. This monitoring typically includes periodic inspections and reappraisals/evaluations. Depending on the type of collateral and the operating cycle, the lender should inspect and reevaluate short-term collateral at least once during the term of the loan. Most Ag lenders are aware of the growing conditions in their trade areas, which gives them a sense of expected borrower crop conditions.

When crops are stored away from the borrower's premises, the bank should be especially careful to confirm the borrower's rights of ownership and possession. For stored commodities, third-party warehouse receipts in the possession of the bank normally provide suitable evidence of the collateral. When products are stored in the borrower's own facilities or in other nonbonded facilities, banks should develop policies and procedures governing how the inventory will be monitored, verified, and controlled based on the borrower's risk profile.

In assessing the value of cash crops on hand, normal practice is to include all harvested crops being held for sale and stored in the farmer's storage facilities, in an elevator, or elsewhere. These harvested crops should be valued using the current market price, unless there is documented evidence that the borrower has a firm, contracted price for the crops, in which case the contracted price should be used. While valuing crops at the current market price generally provides an appropriate current value, current market price may not always be an accurate measure for determining the collateral position because of the volatility of some commodity prices. It may be appropriate to employ some level of historical averaging while also considering current market conditions and future projections. Crops for feeding the borrower's own livestock, and seed intended to be used for the borrower's own planting, should be treated for underwriting purposes as prepaid expenses, not as liquid collateral. Alternatively, verified surplus feed or seed may be treated as a liquid asset because it is not immediately needed to continue operations. The location, amount, and condition of all harvested or "finished" crops should be verified by the lending bank.

Breeding stock normally should be inspected at least annually. Some livestock, such as those being fed to market weight or the offspring from reproduction, are under the borrower's control for less than one year. In these cases, the lender should generally inspect and appraise the collateral at least once during the period of ownership, if feasible. At a minimum, banks should establish procedures to monitor changes in the collateral. For example, in lieu of inspections of larger operations, many banks maintain an in-house running inventory of livestock bought and sold, which they compare with the results of the inspection. To prevent the spread of livestock diseases, there are strict rules regarding entrance and exit from confinement facilities, so livestock and poultry raised in these facilities may not be available for inspection. In these situations, the bank should closely monitor inventory levels using inventory-tracking reports and validate operations on an ongoing basis.

Livestock may be located on the farmer's or rancher's premises, at a third-party feedlot, or elsewhere (such as leased pastureland, public or private). As with crops, the lender should confirm the borrower's rights of ownership and possession. Values can be obtained from numerous sources; trade publications and purchase bills from sale barns are commonly used. Because livestock values may vary dramatically, depending on factors such as the animal's age, health, breed, sex, and reproductive capacity, the individuals performing livestock inspections should be capable of recognizing these issues, making appropriate adjustments, and documenting the results. The bank should determine the amount owed for feeding and housing livestock, as this amount may be subject to an agister's lien, which is typically a priority lien. The bank should also consider liquidation expenses associated with transporting and marketing livestock or grain as part of the collateral valuation process.

Machinery and Equipment

Non-real estate collateral supporting term debt should be inspected and valued periodically. Collateral condition and marketability should be included in the inspection documentation. Analysis of equipment condition should include a supported estimate of depreciation in value resulting from the amount and type of use. A marketability analysis should consider the local supply and demand for similar equipment. Some farm equipment is adaptable to a wide variety of uses, which improves marketability by increasing the number of potential buyers in the event of collateral liquidation. Conversely, other machinery and equipment may be highly specialized or not commonly used in a particular area, and thus not as marketable. A common valuation source for used equipment is the *Farm Equipment Official Guide.* Also, local auctioneers and equipment dealers are often reliable sources of information.

Agricultural Real Estate

The appraisal or evaluation approaches used for Ag real estate are the same as those techniques used to value other types of real estate and are governed by subpart C of 12 CFR 34 (national banks) and 12 CFR 164 (federal savings associations). National banks and federal savings associations are also subject to a uniform rule on real estate lending documented in subpart D of 12 CFR 34 and 12 CFR 160.101. Ag loans secured by real estate must comply with these regulations in applicable situations. The "Commercial Real Estate Lending" booklet of the *Comptroller's Handbook* contains additional information on real estate lending standards.

Events or economic changes may cause farm and ranch real estate values to fluctuate subsequent to the bank's valuations. When this occurs, prudent risk management may require updated collateral valuations. Depending on the borrower's relative financial strength and the bank's reliance on the underlying collateral, an approximate market value based on the banker's knowledge of local market conditions may be adequate. If, however, a federally related transaction has occurred, the transaction is subject to the applicable appraisal regulation.

Credit Administration

Ongoing Monitoring

Ongoing monitoring is a critical component of the vigilance necessary to ensure prudent Ag lending. This requires not only remaining abreast of the borrower's operations, but also keeping up with market events that may affect the borrower. The bank should regularly monitor crop and livestock development and compare it to assumptions provided in the budget or cash flow projection. When there is significant deviation, a new or updated analysis should be considered. The bank should also assess current market prices and the discount rate in comparison with prior assumptions. The updated lender analysis should be documented and should consider whether the borrower's ability to repay debt has deteriorated to a point below the bank's underwriting standards.

The quality of financial information and subsequent analysis is an integral part of any Ag credit. This analysis should include

- determining the adequacy of cash flow to service debt.
- determining compliance with any financial covenants contained in the loan agreement.
- reviewing the reasonableness of budget assumptions and projections.
- comparing projections with actual results.
- assessing and documenting crop or livestock development.
- determining the effect of crop or livestock perils from weather, disease, or pests.
- analyzing net worth and leverage changes.
- updating changes in collateral value.
- assessing the effect of capital expenses.

Sensitivity analysis in the underwriting process should estimate the effect of changes to the borrower's primary and secondary repayment ability. Updates to both the base case and sensitivity case analyses should be performed at least annually. As in the underwriting sensitivity analysis, loan repayment should fall within the standards set by the bank's policy.

Exception Monitoring

Similar to other types of lending, a bank should have a system to monitor Ag loans that involve more liberal underwriting than the lending policy or practices would normally permit. The bank should have a process to identify, approve, document, and monitor these exceptions. Additionally, the bank should track exceptions, such as deterioration in repayment capacity or collateral values, on an ongoing basis. To gain the maximum benefit from such a process, bank management information systems (MIS) should provide data not only on individual exceptions, but also on the aggregate portfolio level. Such aggregated data can provide a more complete picture of risk in the portfolio and reveal weaknesses in the underwriting process, or in the policy itself, that may need to be addressed.

Concentrations

Management should consider the potential effect on earnings and capital and on the bank's operating strategy from Ag lending under stressed market or economic conditions. When a pool of Ag loans is sensitive to the same economic, financial, or business development factors, the entire pool may perform as if it were a single, large exposure when those factors change. History shows that concentrations in Ag loans coupled with depressed markets can contribute to significant credit losses even where underwriting practices are strong. It is important that risk management practices be commensurate with the bank's risk profile and continue to evolve with increasing Ag credit concentrations.

Banks are encouraged to stratify their Ag portfolios into segments that reflect common sensitivities for purposes of identifying concentrations. For example, the bank may segment its Ag portfolio by collateral type, geographic market, crop or livestock type, dryland or irrigated farming, whether operated by tenant or owner, and risk rating. Other useful stratifications may include loan structure, loan purpose, loan-to-value, debt service coverage, policy exceptions on newly underwritten credit facilities, and affiliated loans. Because of correlations among Ag-related risk factors, stress testing can be an important part of the bank's risk management process. Further guidance is contained in the "Concentrations of Credit" booklet of the *Comptroller's Handbook*.

Environmental Issues

Environmental contamination may negatively affect the value of real property collateral as well as create potential liability for a bank under various environmental laws. Ag loans secured by real property may expose the bank to environmentally related risks. Additionally, some Ag industries are more highly regulated for environmental contamination (see the "Compliance" and "Reputation Risk" sections of this booklet for details and examples). Therefore, the bank's Ag loan policy should establish a program for assessing the potential adverse effect of environmental contamination and ensure appropriate controls are in place to limit the bank's exposure to environmental liability associated with real estate taken as collateral.

If determined to be a responsible party or owner of repossessed property after foreclosure, the bank may be held financially responsible for environmental remediation under provisions of the Comprehensive Environmental Response, Compensation, and Liability Act (42 USC 9601 et seq.). Further, significant environmental disasters can severely increase reputation risk for responsible parties—including a bank financing Ag lending. As a result, potential liabilities can greatly exceed the amount of the original loan. The bank should perform appropriate due diligence to understand and evaluate any existing environmental issues and potential environmental risks. Both the borrower's operations and loan collateral should be considered in this analysis.

Audit and Loan Review Function

The board should ensure that the internal audit functions are independent of Ag loan production, approval, and credit administration functions. Internal audit and loan review performance evaluations (or approved lists, when using third-party auditors or loan review firms), should also be completed by someone independent of the loan approval process. Further, the compensation program for auditors and loan review personnel should not include incentives for Ag loan volume generated by the lending department.

Loan review is a critical control function. Periodic objective reviews of the Ag portfolio provide an assessment of credit risk and risk management processes. Loan review should be effective in identifying risk management weaknesses and should provide the bank with sufficient information to address concerns as they emerge. Weaknesses in the loan review process may hamper the entire portfolio management process.

Allowance for Loan and Lease Losses

The bank should segment Ag loans with similar characteristics in its ALLL analyses when there is a significant concentration. For example, the market conditions and factors that affect crop loans differ somewhat from those that affect livestock loans. Both of these portfolios lend themselves to treatment as separate pools in the ALLL analysis. When changes or adverse conditions (such as poor weather conditions) pose additional risks, the bank should consider adjusting historical loss rates to ensure an adequately funded ALLL. In addition, the ALLL analysis should consider the level and risk associated with any carryover debt. Further guidance is contained in the "Allowance for Loan and Lease Losses" booklet of the *Comptroller's Handbook*.

Risk Rating Agricultural Loans

As with other types of loans, Ag loans that are adequately protected by the current sound worth and debt service capacity of the borrower, guarantor, and underlying collateral generally should not be classified. Portions of loans guaranteed by the U.S. government or its agencies should be rated pass, provided all documentation and servicing conditions set forth in the guarantees are met. Additionally, loans to sound borrowers that are refinanced or renewed in accordance with prudent underwriting standards should not be classified unless well-defined weaknesses exist that jeopardize repayment. The bank should not be criticized for continuing to carry loans with weaknesses that resulted in classification or criticism so long as the bank has a well-conceived and effective workout plan for such borrowers and effective internal controls to manage the level of these loans.

When the bank's restructurings are not supported by adequate analysis and documentation, however, examiners are expected to exercise reasonable judgment in reviewing and determining loan classifications until the bank is able to provide information to support management's conclusions and internal loan grades.

When evaluating Ag loans for possible classification, examiners should apply the uniform classification definitions found in the "Rating Credit Risk" booklet of the *Comptroller's Handbook*. To determine the appropriate risk rating, examiners should consider all information relevant to evaluating the prospects that the loan will be repaid. This includes information on the borrower's creditworthiness, the value of (and cash flow provided by) all collateral supporting the loan, and any support provided by financially responsible guarantors.

There are no mandatory rules to direct examiners how to treat Ag credit. Instead, each lending relationship should be analyzed to determine how its individual characteristics compare with the following key criteria:

- Borrower's financial condition, e.g., liquidity, leverage, cash flow, and free assets.
- Whether the loan is performing according to reasonable repayment terms.
- Whether collateral is sufficiently liquid, valuable, and controlled to fully protect the loan if the borrower defaults. (Consider the cost of liquidating collateral.)
- Borrower's historical farming and borrowing performance.
- Other strengths (e.g., crop insurance, significant guarantors, or family support) not previously mentioned that mitigate loan criticism.

Although none of these criteria individually determines the appropriate supervisory treatment of any farm loan, positive determinations to most or all of them would indicate a likelihood that the loan should be passed by examiners. Conversely, negative determinations to most or all would indicate an increased likelihood that the loan deserves some degree of criticism.

The following guidelines for classifying a troubled Ag loan apply when repayment of the debt will be provided solely by the underlying collateral and there are no other available and reliable sources of repayment:

- As a general principle, any portion of the loan balance that exceeds the value of the collateral and can clearly be identified as uncollectible should be classified loss.
- The portion of the loan balance that exceeds the value of the collateral should be classified doubtful when the potential for full loss may be mitigated by the outcome of certain pending events, or when loss is expected but the amount of the loss cannot be reasonably determined.
- The portion of the loan balance that is adequately secured by the value of the collateral should generally be classified no worse than substandard.

Crop Production Loans

Perhaps the most volatile form of Ag lending is short-term production credit. Normally, production loans are self-liquidating, with repayment of the loan occurring shortly after harvest from sale of the crop. When a bank has a reasonable process to analyze projected cash flow, and the projected cash flow indicates the borrower has the ability to repay the operating loan, the current year operating notes are normally rated pass.

When operations have deteriorated and it becomes apparent that the current operating cycle will not result in sufficient production to cover the bank's operating loans, the decision to classify the loan and the severity of classification should begin with a review of the primary collateral, the financial strength of the borrower, and any other sources of repayment.

The amount of collateral represented by cash crops being held for future sale is considered liquid if the value is properly documented with a current market price, the lien is perfected, and the location is verified. Any loans, or portions of loans, covered by this collateral are rated pass.

The proper classification for any portion not covered by liquid collateral depends on the borrower's repayment capacity and the value of any other collateral.

Carryover Debt

By its nature, carryover debt suggests a well-defined credit weakness; it is important, however, for the bank to understand which part of an operating line is true carryover debt. Examiners should not automatically classify carryover debt and should carefully examine all relevant data to ensure an accurate rating. Some factors may lead a farmer not to pay off operating lines while not resulting in carryover debt. For example, a farmer who has a strong crop year may delay crop sales or prepay expenses to reduce income tax liability. While a balance may be left on the operating line at renewal, this would not be an indication of carryover debt. Examiners should consider the following factors when analyzing carryover debt:

- Size of the carryover debt in relation to the size of the borrower's operation.
- Whether the borrower can amortize the carryover debt within a realistic time frame while reasonably servicing all other debt obligations.
- Borrower's historical cash flow, liquidity, and leverage, to assess the ability to absorb carryover debt and the potential for reasonable debt restructuring.

Bank management should have processes in place to determine whether a farm borrower has carryover debt for the current crop year. A best practice is to segregate operating notes by crop year and not comingle operating proceeds between the different growing seasons. If loan proceeds are comingled for more than one crop year, management should be able to document the operating proceeds for each year to support management's risk ratings and repayment analysis.

When collateral does not cover carryover debt and repayment capacity is not evidenced, the carryover balance should be classified and the examiner needs to determine whether a loss rating is appropriate.

Livestock Loans

Loans to feeder livestock operations are expected to be self-liquidating. If a feeder operation deteriorates and the loans warrant classification, the portion of the loans covered by the liquidation value of the feeders should be rated pass if there is a current, on-site livestock inspection report detailing the number of livestock, weight, and current market value. Because livestock values can be volatile and the movement of livestock is relatively easy, the frequency of independent inspections should increase commensurate with the severity of the borrower's financial problems to protect against fraud.

Risk rating loans for financing breeding livestock or dairy cattle is similar to that of feeder loans. Although the primary source of repayment for such loans is the successful reproduction of the livestock or milk sales, the underlying liquidation value of the breeding or dairy livestock provides the same type of readily marketable, liquid collateral support as for feeder livestock.

As with crop loans, secondary sources of repayment, such as additional collateral, may limit the severity of any classified portion.

Equipment Loans

Loans to finance machinery and equipment are capital debt. Equipment loans should be supported and serviced from profitable operations, including any rental income derived from the equipment. These loans should be structured to ensure repayment within the useful life of the equipment. If the debt is paying as agreed, according to a reasonable repayment program, and the source of repayment is generated through profitable operations, the debt would usually be rated pass.

Additional investigation is warranted when equipment loans are being paid with advances on short-term operating loans when operations are not sufficiently profitable. In these situations, a thorough analysis of repayment capacity is required, and the debt should be considered for classification.

When classifying collateral-dependent equipment loans, it is important to have current, documented values for all pieces of equipment, including the date and source of valuation. Independent appraisals are preferable, but values provided by management are acceptable if sufficiently documented. If the collateral values support outstanding balances, a substandard classification is normally appropriate.

If the value of the collateral does not fully protect the debt, a loss classification should be considered for the residual balance unless the debtor has the ability to provide additional security or an alternate source of repayment.

Examination Procedures

This booklet contains expanded procedures for examining specialized activities or specific products or services that warrant extra attention beyond the core assessment contained in the "Community Bank Supervision," "Large Bank Supervision," and "Federal Branches and Agencies Supervision" booklets of the *Comptroller's Handbook*. Examiners determine which expanded procedures to use, if any, during examination planning or after drawing preliminary conclusions during the core assessment.

Scope

These procedures are designed to help examiners tailor the examination to each bank and determine the scope of the Ag lending examination. This determination should consider work performed by internal and external auditors and other independent risk control functions and by other examiners on related areas. Examiners need to perform only those objectives and steps that are relevant to the scope of the examination as determined by the following objective. Seldom will every objective or step of the expanded procedures be necessary.

Objective: To determine the scope of the examination of Ag lending and identify examination objectives and activities necessary to meet the needs of the supervisory strategy for the bank.

1. Review the following sources of information and note any previously identified problems related to Ag lending that require follow-up:

   - Supervisory strategy.
   - Examiner-in-charge's (EIC) scope memorandum.
   - OCC's information system.
   - Previous reports of examination (ROE) and work papers.
   - Loan review reports and work papers.
   - Internal and external audit reports and work papers.
   - Bank management's responses to previous ROEs, loan review reports, and audit reports.
   - Bank correspondence pertaining to Ag lending.
   - Customer complaints and litigation.

2. Obtain the results of reports such as the Uniform Bank Performance Report (UBPR) and Canary. Identify any concerns, trends, or changes involving Ag lending since the last examination. Examiners should be alert to growth rates, changes in portfolio composition, loan yields, and other factors that may affect credit risk.

3. Obtain and review policies, procedures, and reports bank management uses to supervise Ag lending, including internal risk assessments. Consider the following:

   - Portfolio strategies, risk appetite, and risk management guidelines.
   - Loan trial balance, past-due accounts, and loans in nonaccrual status.

- Loan commitment and pipeline reports showing commitments and undisbursed funds.
- Internal loan review reports.
- Credit risk rating reports, including a list of watch credits.
- Problem loan reports for adversely rated Ag loans.
- Customers with carryover debt for the most recent year as well as previous years, including the dollar amount of carryover and loans that contain carryover.
- Concentration of Ag credit reports and board-approved concentration limits.
- Loan policy exception report.
- Financial statement and collateral exception reports.
- Financial statement tracking reports.
- Board and loan committee reports and minutes related to Ag lending activities.
- Loans with terms modified by a reduction of the interest rate or principal payment, by a deferral of interest or principal, or by other restructuring of payment terms.
- Loans with interest capitalized subsequent to initial underwriting.
- Over-disbursed loans.
- Loan participations purchased and sold since the previous examination.
- Shared National Credits, if applicable.
- Organizational chart of the Ag lending department or Ag lending specialist reporting lines, if applicable.
- Résumés of the Ag lending department management and internal loan review staff, including any staff added since the last examination.
- Loans to insiders of the bank or any affiliate of the bank.

4. In discussions with bank management, determine whether there have been any significant changes since the prior examination of Ag lending. Discussions should address

- management's strategy for the Ag lending function, including
  - growth goals.
  - existing and potential sources of loan demand.
  - new loan types, property types, or geographic regions.
  - new marketing strategies and initiatives.
- staff's experience and ability to implement strategic initiatives and achieve goals.
- current and projected concentrations of credit, as well as management's plans to manage concentrations.
- significant changes in policies, procedures, underwriting, personnel, or control systems.
- internal or external factors that can affect the portfolio.
- stress-testing practices.
- observations from examiner review of internal bank reports, as well as OCC and other third-party-generated reports.
- extent of syndicated distribution and participation activities as a buyer and a seller, if applicable.

5. Based on an analysis of information obtained in the previous steps, as well as input from the EIC, determine the scope and objectives of the Ag lending examination. Consider

- growth and acquisitions.
- board or management changes.
- changes in third-party relationships.
- changes in risk limits, including concentrations.
- changes in external factors, such as
  - national, regional, and local economies.
  - industry outlook.
  - regulatory framework.
  - technological changes.

6. Select from the following examination procedures the necessary steps to meet examination objectives and the supervisory strategy.

Quantity of Risk

Conclusion: The quantity of credit and other associated risks is (low, moderate, or high).

The quantity of risk considers the inherent level or volume of risk. Consider the "Quantity of Credit Risk Indicators" in appendix A of this booklet, as appropriate.

Credit Risk

Objective: To determine the quantity of credit risk associated with Ag lending by assessing the product mix, markets, geographies, technologies, volumes, size of the exposures, quality metrics, and concentrations.

1. Analyze the composition of and changes to the Ag portfolio, including off-balance-sheet exposure, since the previous examination. Determine the implications for the quantity of risk from the following:

    - Any significant growth.
    - Material changes in the portfolio, including
        - changes and trends in problem, classified, past-due, nonaccrual, and nonperforming assets; charge-off volumes; and risk-rating distribution.
        - any significant concentrations.
        - Ag portfolios acquired from other institutions.

2. Assess the effect of external factors, including economic, industry, competitive, and market conditions.

3. Assess the effect of potential legislative, regulatory, accounting, and technological changes.

4. Select a sample of loans to be reviewed. Selection of the sample should be consistent with the examination objectives, supervisory strategy, and district business plans. Refer to the "Sampling Methodologies" booklet of the *Comptroller's Handbook* for guidance on sampling techniques. Consider

    - new large loans.
    - new loan types.
    - loans originated in new geographic regions.
    - loans at or above the legal lending limit.
    - loans to insiders of the bank or any affiliates.
    - over-disbursed loans.
    - loans with multiple extensions.
    - special mention or classified loans.

- loans identified as having carryover that are not adversely risk rated by the bank.
- loans with significant policy or underwriting exceptions.
- loans with modified repayment terms.
- concentration reports.
- portfolio stress-testing reports.

5. Obtain and review credit files for all borrowers in the sample and prepare line sheets for the sampled credits. Line sheets should contain sufficient analysis to determine the credit rating; support any criticisms of underwriting, servicing, or credit administration practices; and document any violations of law. In particular, file readers should

- evaluate the quality of underwriting, if the loan was originated, renewed, or restructured in the last 12 months. Consider whether the approval document is consistent with the bank's underwriting policy.
- determine the primary source of repayment of each loan and evaluate the primary source's adequacy.
- assess the adequacy of cash flow to meet debt service requirements.
- comment as necessary regarding historical trends in production levels and income to cover operating expenses.
- evaluate budgeted expenses, including the level and trend of capital expenditures, anticipated working capital needs, and significant costs for any necessary capital replacement or repair.
- analyze secondary sources of repayment provided by guarantors, financial sponsors, or endorsers. If the borrower's financial condition warrants concern, determine the guarantor's, sponsor's, or endorser's capacity and willingness to repay the credit.
- determine the effect of hedging and when hedging will be required, where applicable.
- determine the effect of any mitigating insurance coverage or government guarantees. Evaluate whether conditions and documentation are in place to ensure payment of insurance or guarantees should a claim be necessary.
- evaluate the effect of changes to technology, government regulations, current price levels, or economic markets, where applicable.
- compare collateral with the description on the collateral register.
- determine that items such as property assignments, stock powers, hypothecation agreement, or statements of purpose are on file.
- test the pricing of negotiable collateral, if applicable.
- list all collateral discrepancies and investigate.
- evaluate the due diligence performed to assess environmental risk.
- determine whether crop and livestock inspections have been completed and documented. Evaluate the quality and independence of the inspections and whether verification of ownership was documented.
- evaluate sufficiency of collateral coverage. Determine whether the appraisals or evaluations on real estate were obtained consistent with regulatory requirements (12 CFR 34, subpart C, for national banks and 12 CFR 164 for federal savings associations) and meet Uniform Standards of Professional Appraisal Practice.

- determine whether appraisals and inspections of significant machinery and equipment are present. Evaluate whether wear and damage were assessed.
- determine whether the borrower complies with the loan agreement and financial covenants.
- evaluate sensitivity analysis. Assess the effect of changes to the borrower's primary and secondary repayment ability. Compare updates to both the base case and sensitivity case analyses to the standards set in the bank's policy.
- document all significant loan policy, loan administration, and underwriting exceptions and determine whether the exceptions were appropriately identified, approved, and reported.
- determine any significant structural weaknesses and the effect on the borrower's ability to repay on reasonable terms.
- assign risk ratings to the sampled credits. Refer to risk-rating guidance in this booklet and supervisory guidance regarding risk ratings.

6. Review the completed line sheets and summarize the loan sample results. The examiner responsible for the Ag lending review should

- if applicable, identify recommended loan risk rating downgrades and ensure such decisions are appropriately documented.
- maintain a list of structurally weak loans reviewed.
- maintain a list of loans for which examiners were unable to determine the risk rating due to a lack of information.
- maintain a list of loans not supported by current and complete financial information and for which collateral documentation is deficient.
- summarize whether policy, underwriting, loan administration, or documentation exceptions were appropriately identified and approved.

7. Analyze the level, composition, and trend of policy and underwriting exceptions and determine the effect on the quantity of risk. Consider the frequency of reporting, total dollar volume, percentage of the portfolio and percentage of total capital that exceptions represent in comparison with established limits. (Note: A bank's lack of an internal tracking system indicates a need to test for adherence to policy.)

8. Evaluate the trend and level of concentrations of Ag credit. Consider exposure as a percentage of total capital compared with policy limits for particular crops, products, geographies, or related borrowers.

9. Evaluate portfolio stress testing. Determine whether assumptions to develop base case and downside case are reasonable and whether key vulnerabilities have been considered.

10. Determine whether any previously charged-off Ag loans were re-booked.

11. Using a list of nonaccruing loans, test loan accrual records to confirm that interest income is not recorded after the loan has been placed on nonaccrual.

---

12. Evaluate the adequacy of the Ag portfolio's ALLL.

13. Review "Quantity of Credit Risk Indicators" (appendix A) in this booklet, as appropriate.

14. Discuss the results of the loan sample with the EIC or examiner responsible for loan portfolio management (LPM) and bank management.

Other Associated Risks

In addition to credit risk, Ag lending can generate interest rate risk, liquidity risk, operational risk, compliance risk, strategic risk, and reputation risk. These risks and the ways Ag lending can expose the bank to these risks are discussed in the "Introduction" section of this booklet.

Objective: To determine the quantity of other risks associated with Ag lending activities.

1. Assess the quantity of interest rate risk associated with Ag lending. Consider

   - effect of interest rate changes on both the borrowers and the bank.
   - underwriting terms such as tenor and management's pricing structure, e.g., fixed vs. variable interest rates and the potential exposure to different pricing indices.
   - off-balance-sheet exposures.
   - quality and results of sensitivity analysis and portfolio stress testing.

2. Assess the quantity of liquidity risk associated with Ag lending. Consider

   - Ag portfolio growth rates and the corresponding funding strategies.
   - composition and trends of the Ag portfolio and the ability to convert the loans to cash. Consider correlated concentrations of Ag-related assets and liabilities that may be subject to similar supply and demand volatility.
   - current market conditions, including
     - longer-term liquidity pressure due to population migration, depressed commodity prices, weather-related disasters, or crop or livestock epidemics.
     - deposit trends in regions dependent on the Ag economy.

3. Assess the quantity of operational risk associated with Ag lending. Consider

   - any operational losses resulting from the Ag lending function.
   - control weaknesses identified by audit, loan review, or any other control group.
   - quality of board oversight.
   - quality of the loan approval and underwriting process.
   - quality of credit administration, e.g., segregation of duties, financial analysis, monitoring, and documentation standards.
   - quality and independence of the appraisal and collateral valuation functions.
   - quality and independence of the audit and loan review functions.
   - staffing turnover affecting the Ag lending function.

- responses to the internal control questionnaire (ICQ).

4. Assess the quantity of compliance risk associated with Ag lending. Consider

- the bank's history of compliance with lending related laws and regulations, particularly those regarding appraisals, insider-lending activities, legal lending limits, and affiliates, as well as safe and sound banking practices.
- for federal savings associations, whether Ag loans are approaching the limits described in 12 USC 1464(c)(2)(A) and 12 CFR 160.30. Ag loans typically are classified as commercial loans, which, under 12 USC 1464(c)(2)(A), cannot exceed 20 percent of total assets. Within that limit, amounts in excess of 10 percent of assets are used only for small business loans. Small business loans include any loan to a small business (defined in 12 CFR 160.3 and 13 CFR 121) and any loan that does not exceed $2 million and is for commercial, corporate, business, or agricultural purposes. A federal savings association, however, may make Ag loans under other authority, depending on the circumstances. For example, to the extent nonresidential real property secures an Ag loan, a federal savings association may make the loan under its nonresidential loan authority. Under this authority, a federal savings association generally may make loans secured by nonresidential real property up to 400 percent of capital.
- the quality of the bank's environmental risk management program and losses attributed to liabilities resulting from environmental risk.
- compliance with internal policies and procedures.

5. Assess the level of strategic risk associated with Ag lending. Consider

- management's strategy regarding Ag lending and the potential effect on risks including concentrations of credit.
- board oversight of strategic initiatives and stated risk appetite and risk limits as a percentage of total capital.
- the adequacy of the bank's program for monitoring economic and market conditions. Consider management's assessment of Ag commodity supply and demand, government policies, and socioeconomic and demographic trends.
- ability of the staff to effectively implement Ag lending strategies without exposing the bank to unwarranted risk.

6. Assess the level of reputation risk associated with Ag lending. Consider

- the bank's effectiveness in meeting the Ag lending needs of the communities it serves, including credit needs of small businesses that depend on the Ag industry.
- management's oversight of environmental compliance and social responsibility efforts to limit negative public perception and lender liability as they pertain to Ag lending.
- the bank's effectiveness in working with stressed borrowers and the Ag community during periods of economic or financial stress.

- management's oversight of large or complex Ag lending relationships that affect the local economy.

Quality of Risk Management

Conclusion: The quality of risk management is (strong, satisfactory, or weak).

Determine the quality of risk management considering all risks associated with Ag lending. Consider the "Quality of Credit Risk Management Indicators" in appendix B of this booklet, as appropriate.

Policies

Policies are statements of actions adopted by a bank to pursue certain objectives. Policies often set standards and should be consistent with the bank's underlying mission, values, and principles. A policy review should always be triggered when the bank's objectives or standards change.

Objective: To determine the adequacy of Ag loan policies. Consider whether the policies address the following:

1. Loan structures permitted and how maximum loan amounts are determined.

2. Maximum advance rates or minimum collateral margins for machinery and equipment.

3. Maximum advance rates or minimum collateral margins for all categories of crops and livestock in production.

4. Frequency of inspections and collateral revaluations.

5. Frequency and timing of budget or cash flow projection variance analysis.

6. How credit enhancements are used to support credit underwriting, including

   - FSA programs.
   - insurance policies.
   - U.S. Small Business Administration programs.
   - state-level programs.
   - personal guarantees.

7. Maximum loan term and whether the term reflects the purpose of the loan and source of repayment.

8. Whether the policy establishes guidance for monitoring hedging strategies, forward contracting, third-party contracts, and timing of cash market sales.

9. Required documentation and filings.

---

10. Environmental risk.

11. How Ag loan policy exceptions are defined, identified, monitored, and controlled, including expectations for the frequency of exception report updates. Has the bank established a limit for the percentage of the portfolio with exceptions and does the board of directors monitor the bank's performance against this limit?

12. Annual board review and approval of the Ag lending policy. Does the board

    • evaluate existing policies to determine whether they are compatible with market conditions?
    • update stress-testing requirements for borrowers, including the minimum loan size that will require management to perform stress tests on an individual borrower?
    • review stress-testing policy on the entire Ag loan portfolio and on individual related segments of the Ag portfolio?
    • ensure policies are consistent with the bank's strategic direction and risk appetite?

Processes

Processes are the procedures, programs, and practices that impose order on a bank's pursuit of its objectives. Processes define how daily activities are carried out. Effective processes are consistent with the underlying policies and are governed by appropriate checks and balances (such as internal controls).

Objective: To assess the adequacy of the bank's lending practices, procedures, and internal controls regarding Ag loans.

1. Evaluate how policies, procedures, and plans affecting the Ag portfolio are communicated. Consider whether

    • management has clearly communicated objectives and risk limits as a percentage of total capital for the Ag portfolio to the board of directors and whether the board has approved these goals.
    • communication to key personnel in the Ag department is clear and timely.

2. Determine whether MIS, including exception reports, inspection reports, and commodity pricing reports, provide timely, useful information to evaluate risk levels and trends in the Ag portfolio.

3. Assess the process management uses to ensure the accuracy and integrity of Ag loan data.

    • Is there a process to compare production and expenses from previous budget or cash flow projections to actual production and expenses for the same period?

4. Determine the effectiveness of processes to monitor compliance with the Ag policy. Consider

    - approval and monitoring of policy limit exceptions.
    - volume and type of exceptions, including any identified in the loan sample.
    - internal loan review, audit, and compliance process findings.

5. Assess the underwriting process for Ag lending. Consider

    - appropriateness of the approval process, including officers' approval limits.
    - quality of the loan approval documents. Do they contain the following?
        - Industry analysis.
        - Adequate description of the nature, size, and complexity of the farmer's or rancher's operations, including management depth and experience.
        - Comprehensive financial analysis of the borrower and any guarantors, including repayment capacity and financial projections.
        - Support for the loan structure, including loan term, amortization schedule, pricing, loan amount, advance rates, and, if applicable, loan covenants.
        - Identification of loan policy exceptions and any mitigating factors.
        - Identification of key risks and any mitigating factors.
        - Purpose of loan.
        - Primary and secondary sources of repayment.
        - Description of collateral and lien status.
        - Environmental risk factors.
        - Budget or cash flow projection summary, including support for significant budget exceptions.
        - Stress testing.
        - Support for the assigned risk rating.
        - Upgrade and downgrade triggers for lowest pass and criticized grades.

6. Evaluate the accuracy and integrity of the internal risk-rating processes. Consider

    - findings from the loan sample.
    - role of internal loan review.

7. Determine whether there are processes to monitor strategic and business plans for the Ag portfolio. Consider

    - effect on earnings and capital if the Ag portfolio business plans and strategies are executed.

8. Assess the process to ensure compliance with applicable laws, rulings, regulations, and environmental guidelines.

- Consider special environmental guidelines pertaining to certain types of Ag production (such as hog farms, dairy farms, or aquaculture), if applicable.

9. Evaluate the effectiveness of processes used to monitor Ag collateral. Consider the following questions:

   - For equipment loans, are values updated periodically?
   - Does the bank have adequate processes to monitor Ag prices?
   - Evaluate the effectiveness of collateral monitoring. Consider the quality, timing, and independence of the appraisal and appraisal review functions and inspections, and management's criteria for updating or obtaining new valuations and inspections throughout the life of the loan.
     - For livestock loans,
       - are inspections performed, at a minimum, annually?
       - is there a breakdown by sex, breed, and number in each category?
       - is the condition of each animal noted?
       - are published livestock prices used to prepare cash flow projections?
     - For crop loans,
       - are inspections of growing crops performed as the loans are advanced?
       - does the bank monitor local and regional crop yields?
       - are published commodity prices used for cash flow projections?
       - if published commodity prices are not used, does the bank document the support for its prices?
   - Does the bank have processes to ensure that liens on Ag properties are properly filed and perfected?
   - Does the bank have processes to monitor the adequacy of insurance coverage?

10. The examiner reviewing the Ag lending portfolio should review the LPM examiner's findings to determine whether additional analysis is required for issues related to Ag lending pertaining to

    - problem credit administration.
    - collections.
    - charge-offs.

11. Review the methodology for evaluating and maintaining the ALLL.

    - Consider whether the portfolio is analyzed as a separate pool or further segmented by loan type (for example, crops, livestock, irrigated land, dryland, or equipment) or by geographic area.
    - Is the methodology reasonable based on historical experience and current trends?

12. Verify that the bank has an effective process to periodically evaluate internal controls. (Note: The lack of an effective process may require examiners to conduct additional testing, such as completing the Internal Control Questionnaire.)

Personnel

Personnel are the bank staff and managers who execute or oversee processes. Personnel should be qualified and competent, and should perform appropriately. They should understand the bank's mission, values, principles, policies, and processes. Banks should design compensation programs to attract, develop, and retain qualified personnel. In addition, compensation programs should be structured in a manner that encourages strong risk management practices.

Objective: To determine whether management and Ag lending and administrative personnel possess and display acceptable knowledge and technical skills to manage and perform their duties, given the size and complexity of the bank.

1. Evaluate the adequacy of the Ag lending staff in terms of the level of expertise and number of assigned personnel. Consider

   - whether staffing levels support current operations or any planned growth.
   - staff turnover.
   - staff's previous Ag lending and workout experience.
   - specialized training provided.
   - average account load per lending officer and whether loads are reasonable in light of the complexity and condition of each officer's portfolio.
   - how senior management and the board of directors periodically evaluate Ag lenders' understanding of and conformance with the bank's stated credit culture and loan policy. If there is no process, determine the effect on the management of credit risk.
   - adequacy of training, development, and succession planning.

2. Assess the performance management and compensation programs for Ag lending personnel. Consider whether these programs measure and reward behaviors that support strategic and risk objectives for the portfolio.

   If the bank offers incentive compensation programs, determine whether they are consistent with OCC Bulletin 2010-24, "Interagency Guidance on Sound Incentive Compensation Policies," including compliance with its three key principles: (1) Provide employees with incentives that appropriately balance risk and reward; (2) Be compatible with effective controls and risk management; and (3) Be supported by strong corporate governance, including active and effective oversight by the bank's board of directors.

3. If the bank has third-party relationships that involve critical activities, determine whether oversight is consistent with OCC Bulletin 2013-29, "Third-Party Relationships: Risk Management Guidance."

Control Systems

Control systems are the functions (such as internal and external audits, risk review, and quality assurance) and information systems that bank managers use to measure performance, make decisions about risk, and assess the effectiveness of processes. Control functions should have clear reporting lines, adequate resources, and appropriate authority. MIS should provide timely, accurate, and relevant feedback.

Objective: To determine whether the bank has systems in place to provide accurate and timely assessments of the risks associated with its Ag lending activities.

1. Evaluate the effectiveness of monitoring systems to identify, measure, and track Ag concentrations and exceptions to policies and established limits.

2. Determine whether MIS provides timely, accurate, and useful information to evaluate risk levels and trends in the bank's Ag lending activities.

3. Assess the scope, frequency, effectiveness, and independence of the internal and external audits of the Ag lending function. Consider the qualifications of audit personnel and evaluate accessibility to necessary information and board responses to audit findings.

4. Assess the effectiveness of loan review. Evaluate the scope, frequency, effectiveness, and independence of loan review, as well as loan review's ability to identify and report emerging risks. Determine whether loan review reports address

   - quality of the Ag loan portfolio.
   - trends in portfolio quality.
   - effectiveness of the underwriting process.
   - quality of loan administration.
   - quality of individual loan and portfolio stress testing.
   - quality of significant relationships.
   - level and trend of policy, underwriting, and pricing exceptions.

Conclusions

Conclusion: The aggregate level of each associated risk is (low, moderate, or high).
The direction of each associated risk is (increasing, stable, or decreasing).

Objective: To determine, document, and communicate overall findings and conclusions regarding the examination of Ag lending.

1. Determine preliminary examination findings and conclusions and discuss with the EIC, including

   - quantity of associated risks (as noted in the "Introduction" section).
   - quality of risk management.
   - aggregate level and direction of associated risks.
   - overall risk in Ag lending.
   - violations and other concerns.

Summary of Risks Associated With Ag Lending				
Risk category	Quantity of risk (Low, moderate, high)	Quality of risk management (Weak, satisfactory, strong)	Aggregate level of risk (Low, moderate, high)	Direction of risk (Increasing, stable, decreasing)
Credit				
Interest rate				
Liquidity				
Operational				
Compliance				
Strategic				
Reputation				

2. If substantive safety and soundness concerns remain unresolved that may have a material adverse effect on the bank, further expand the scope of the examination by completing verification procedures.

3. Discuss examination findings with bank management, including violations, recommendations, and conclusions about risks and risk management practices. If necessary, obtain commitments for corrective action.

4. Compose conclusion comments, highlighting any issues that should be included in the ROE. If necessary, compose a matters requiring attention comment.

5. Update the OCC's information system and any applicable ROE schedules or tables.

6. Write a memorandum specifically setting out what the OCC should do in the future to effectively supervise Ag lending in the bank, including time periods, staffing, and workdays required.

7. Update, organize, and reference work papers in accordance with OCC policy.

8. Ensure any paper or electronic media that contain sensitive bank or customer information are appropriately disposed of or secured.

Internal Control Questionnaire

An ICQ helps an examiner assess a bank's internal controls for an area. ICQs typically address standard controls that provide day-to-day protection of bank assets and financial records. The examiner decides the extent to which it is necessary to complete or update ICQs during examination planning or after reviewing the findings and conclusions of the core assessment.

Policies

1. Has the board of directors, consistent with its duties and responsibilities, adopted written Ag loan policies that are consistent with safe and sound banking practices and appropriate to the size of the bank and the nature and scope of the bank's operations? In particular, do the bank's policies

    *   identify the geographic areas in which the bank will consider lending?
    *   establish a loan portfolio diversification policy and set limits for Ag loans by type and geographic market as a percentage of total capital?
    *   establish policies for the identification, monitoring, and management of concentrations?
    *   establish policies for stress testing the Ag loan portfolio?
    *   identify appropriate terms and conditions, based on risk, for lending on different types of reserves and equipment?
    *   establish loan origination and approval procedures, both generally and by size and type of loan?
    *   establish prudent underwriting standards that are clear and measurable, including
        - maximum loan amounts by purpose and collateral?
        - maximum loan maturities by purpose and collateral?
        - amortization schedules?
        - margin requirements?
        - individual loan stress-testing requirements?
        - collateral coverage?

2. Has the bank established loan administration and documentation expectations for its Ag portfolio that address

    *   type and frequency of financial statements, including requirements for verification of information provided by the borrower?
    *   type and frequency of budget or cash flow projection and inspection reports and updates, including updates to the expected market price and crop yields?
    *   type and frequency of collateral evaluations and inspections (appraisals and other estimates of value)?
    *   loan closing and disbursement procedures, including the supervised disbursement of proceeds on Ag production loans?
    *   payment processing?

- loan payoffs?
- servicing and participation agreements?
- collection and foreclosure, including
  - delinquency and follow-up procedures?
  - foreclosure timing?
  - extensions and other forms of forbearance?
  - acceptance of deeds in lieu of foreclosure?
  - claims processing (e.g., seeking recovery on a defaulted loan covered by an insurance program)?

3. Are procedures in effect to monitor compliance with the bank's Ag lending policies?

- Are exception loans of significant size reported individually to the board of directors?
- Are the numbers and types of exceptions monitored so that the loan policy and lending practices can be periodically evaluated?
- Are loans in excess of the borrowing base identified?
- Are exceptions monitored by a loan officer?

4. Does the bank effectively monitor conditions in the Ag markets to ensure that Ag lending policies remain appropriate?

5. Do the bank's policies and procedures address each Ag lending product offered by the bank and provide guidance for each category, including, for example, crop production, livestock production, farm real estate, pastures, and equipment?

6. Does the bank have an internal review procedure to determine whether inspection policies and procedures are being followed consistently?

7. Are policies and procedures in place to ensure that inspections are timely, so identification of adverse events is not delayed?

8. Does the inspection documentation support the inspector's conclusions?

9. Are procedures in place to review budgets, budget variances, and assumptions for reasonableness before funds are advanced?

10. Does the bank take steps to determine whether there are any environmental hazards associated with the real estate proposed as collateral?

11. When there is reason to believe that there may be serious environmental problems associated with property it holds as collateral, does the bank

- take steps to monitor the situation to minimize any potential liability on the bank's part?
- seek the advice of experts, particularly when considering foreclosure on a contaminated property?

Ag Underwriting

12. Does the bank require

- current and historical financial statements?
- current and historical tax returns?
- credit checks?

13. Do Ag loan budgets include all costs to bring the crops or livestock to market?

14. Does the bank require an estimated cost breakdown for each expense?

15. Does the bank require that qualified personnel review expansion project cost estimates?

Disbursements

16. Are disbursements

- advanced on a prearranged disbursement plan?
- made only after reviewing invoices, if a disbursement presents a large or unplanned deviation from budget or cash flow projection?
- subject to advance, written authorization by the
  - borrower?
  - lending officer?
- reviewed by a bank employee who had no part in granting the loan?
- compared to original cost estimates?
- checked against previous disbursements?
- made directly to suppliers or vendors?
- made in accordance with the loan agreement?

17. Are periodic reviews of undisbursed loan proceeds completed for adequacy and reconciled to the budget or cash flow projection?

Documentation

18. Does the bank require that documentation files include

- loan applications?
- financial statements for the
  - borrower?
  - guarantors?
- credit and trade checks on the
  - borrower?
  - guarantors?
- copies of all Ag budgets or cash flow projections?

- loan agreement?
- inspection and appraisal reports?
- other supporting valuation documentation, such as an auctioneer's value estimate?
- title searches and other lien searches?
- mortgage?
- financing statements and security agreements?
- disbursement authorizations?
- insurance policies?
- hedging contracts or commitments?
- bank and customer correspondence?

Conclusion

19. Is the foregoing information an adequate basis for evaluating internal control, in that there are no significant additional internal auditing procedures, accounting controls, administrative controls, or other circumstances that impair any controls or mitigate any weaknesses indicated above? (Explain negative answers briefly and indicate conclusions as to their effect on specific examination or verification procedures.)

20. Based on the answers to the foregoing questions, internal control for Ag lending is considered (strong, satisfactory, or weak).

Verification Procedures

Verification procedures are used to verify the existence of assets and liabilities, or test the reliability of financial records. Examiners generally do not perform verification procedures as part of a typical examination. Rather, verification procedures are performed when substantive safety and soundness concerns are identified that are not mitigated by the bank's risk management systems and internal controls.

1. Reconcile the trial balance to the general ledger. Include loan commitments, overdrafts, and other contingent liabilities in the testing.

2. Using an appropriate sampling technique, select loans from the trial balance and do the following:

   - Prepare and mail confirmation forms to borrowers. Loans serviced by other institutions, either whole loans or participations, should be confirmed only with the servicing institution. Loans serviced for other institutions, either whole loans or participations, should be confirmed with the other institution and the borrower. Confirmation forms should include the borrower's name, loan number, original amount, interest rate, current loan balance, contingency or escrow account balance and a brief description of the collateral.
     - After a reasonable time period, mail second requests.
     - Follow up on any no-replies or exceptions and resolve differences.
   - Examine notes for completeness and reconcile date, amount, and terms to trial balance.
     - If any notes are not held at the bank, request confirmation with the holder.
     - See that required initials of approving officer are on the note.
     - See that the note is signed, appears to be genuine, and is negotiable.
   - Compare collateral held in files with the description on the collateral register. List and investigate all collateral discrepancies.
   - Determine whether any collateral is held by an outside custodian or has been temporarily removed for any reason. Request confirmation for any collateral held.
   - Determine whether each file contains documentation supporting guarantees and subordination agreements, where appropriate.
   - Determine whether any required insurance coverage is adequate and that the bank is named as loss payee.
   - Review participation agreements, making excerpts, when deemed necessary, for such items as rate of service fee, interest rate, retention of late charges, and remittance requirements, and determine whether the customer has complied.
   - Review loan agreement provisions for holdback or retention, and determine whether undisbursed loan funds or contingency or escrow accounts are equal to retention or holdback requirements.
     - If separate reserves are maintained, determine whether debit entries to those accounts are authorized in accordance with the terms of the loan agreement and

whether they are supported by inspection reports, individual bills, or other evidence.
- Review disbursement ledgers and authorizations and determine whether authorizations are signed in accordance with the terms of the loan agreement.
- Reconcile debits in the undisbursed loan proceeds accounts to inspection reports, individual bills, or other evidence supporting disbursements.

3. Review the accrued-interest accounts and

- review procedures for accounting for accrued interest and handling of adjustments.
- scan accrued-interest and income accounts for any unusual entries and follow up on any unusual items by tracing to initial and supporting records.

4. Obtain or prepare a schedule showing the amount of monthly interest income and the real estate loan balances at the end of each month since the last examination and

- calculate or check yield.
- investigate significant fluctuations or trends.

5. Using a list of nonaccruing loans, check loan accrual records to determine whether interest income is being accrued.

Appendixes

Appendix A: Quantity of Credit Risk Indicators

Examiners should consider the following indicators when assessing the quantity of credit risk in Ag lending activities.

Low	Moderate	High
The level of Ag loans outstanding is low relative to capital.	The level of Ag loans outstanding is moderate relative to capital.	The level of Ag loans outstanding is high relative to capital.
Ag growth rates are supported by local, regional, or national economic trends. Growth, including off-balance-sheet activities, has been planned for and is commensurate with management and staff expertise, as well as operational capabilities.	Ag growth rates exceed local, regional, or national economic trends. Growth, including off-balance-sheet activities, has not been planned for or exceeds planned levels and may test the capabilities of management, credit staff, and MIS.	Ag growth rates significantly exceed local, regional, or national economic trends. Growth, including off-balance-sheet activities, has not been planned for or exceeds planned levels and stretches the experience and capability of management, credit staff, and MIS. Growth may also be in new products or outside the bank's traditional lending area.
Interest and fee income from Ag lending activities is not a significant portion of loan income.	Interest and fee income from Ag lending activities is an important component of loan income; however, the bank's lending activities remain diversified.	The bank is highly dependent on interest and fees from Ag lending activities. Management may seek higher returns through higher-risk product or customer types. Loan yields may be disproportionate relative to risk.
The bank's Ag portfolio is well diversified, with no single large concentrations or a few moderate concentrations. Concentrations are well within reasonable internal limits. The Ag portfolio mix does not materially affect the risk profile.	The bank has a few material Ag concentrations that may be approaching internal limits. The Ag portfolio mix may increase the bank's credit risk profile.	The bank has large Ag concentrations that may exceed internal limits. The Ag portfolio mix increases the bank's credit risk profile.
Ag underwriting is conservative. Policies and procedures are reasonable. Ag loans with structural weaknesses or underwriting exceptions are occasionally originated; however, the weaknesses are effectively mitigated.	Ag underwriting is satisfactory. The bank has an average level of Ag loans with structural weaknesses. Exceptions are reasonably mitigated and consistent with competitive pressures and reasonable growth objectives.	Ag underwriting is liberal and policies are inadequate. The bank has a high level of Ag loans with structural weaknesses or underwriting exceptions, the volume of which exposes the bank to loss in the event of default.

Low	Moderate	High
Collateral requirements for Ag loans are conservative. Collateral valuations are reasonable, timely, and well supported.	Collateral requirements for Ag loans are acceptable. Some collateral exceptions exist, but are reasonably mitigated and monitored. A moderate volume of collateral valuations are not well supported. Updated collateral valuations are not always obtained in a timely manner.	Collateral requirements for Ag loans are liberal, or if policies are conservative, substantial deviations exist. Collateral valuations are not always obtained, frequently unsupported, or reflect inadequate protection. Updated collateral values are not obtained in a timely manner.
Ag loan documentation or collateral exceptions are low and have minimal effect on the bank's risk profile.	The level of Ag loan documentation or collateral exceptions is moderate; however, exceptions are reasonably mitigated and corrected in a timely manner, if applicable. The risk of loss from these exceptions is not material.	The level of Ag loan documentation or collateral exceptions is high. Exceptions are not mitigated and not corrected in a timely manner. The risk of loss from the exceptions is heightened.
Ag loan distribution across pass category is consistent with a conservative risk appetite. Migration trends within the pass category favor the less risky ratings. Lagging indicators, including past dues and nonaccruals, are low and stable.	Ag distribution across pass category is consistent with a moderate risk appetite. Migration trends within the pass category may favor riskier ratings. Lagging indicators, including past dues and nonaccruals, are moderate and may be slightly increasing.	Ag distribution across the pass category is heavily skewed toward riskier pass ratings. Lagging indicators, including past dues and nonaccruals, are moderate or high and the trend is increasing.
The volume of classified and special mention Ag loans is low and is not skewed toward more severe risk ratings.	The volume of classified and special mention Ag loans is moderate but is not skewed toward more severe ratings.	The volume of classified and special mention Ag loans is moderate or high, skewed to the more severe ratings, and increasing.
Ag refinancing and renewal practices raise little or no concern regarding the quality of Ag loans and the accuracy of reported problem loan data.	Ag refinancing and renewal practices pose some concerns regarding the quality of Ag loans and the accuracy of reported problem loan data.	Ag refinancing and renewal practices raise substantial concerns regarding the quality of Ag loans and the accuracy of reported problem loan data.
The volume of loans secured by Ag with environmental issues is not significant. Environmental analyses are timely, appropriate, and well supported.	A moderate volume of Ag loans with environmental concerns exists; however, the risks are identified and reasonably mitigated. Environmental evaluations are not always performed in a timely manner.	The volume of Ag loans with environmental concerns is material if left uncorrected. Environmental evaluations are not performed in a timely manner or management's response to identified environmental issues is not appropriate.

Appendix B: Quality of Credit Risk Management Indicators

Examiners should consider the following indicators when assessing the quality of credit risk management in Ag lending activities.

Strong	Satisfactory	Weak
There is a clear, sound Ag credit culture. Board and management appetite for risk is well communicated and fully understood.	The intent of Ag lending activities is generally understood, but the culture and risk appetite may not be clearly communicated or uniformly implemented throughout the bank.	The Ag credit culture is absent or materially flawed. Risk appetite may not be well understood.
Ag initiatives are consistent with a conservative risk appetite and promote an appropriate balance between risk taking and strategic objectives. New Ag loan products are well researched, tested, and approved before implementation.	Ag initiatives are consistent with a moderate risk appetite. Generally, there is an appropriate balance between risk taking and strategic objectives; however, anxiety for income may lead to higher-risk transactions. New Ag products may be launched without sufficient testing, but risks are generally understood.	Ag initiatives are liberal and encourage risk taking. Anxiety for income dominates planning activities. The bank introduces new Ag products without conducting sufficient due diligence.
Management is effective. The Ag lending staff possesses sufficient expertise to effectively administer the risk assumed. Responsibilities and accountability are clear, and appropriate remedial or corrective action is taken when they are breached.	Ag risk management is satisfactory, but improvement may be needed in one or more areas. Ag lending staff generally possess the expertise to administer assumed risks; however, additional expertise may be required. Responsibilities and accountability may require some clarification. In general, appropriate remedial or corrective action is taken when they are breached.	Ag risk management is deficient. Ag lending staff may not possess sufficient expertise or may demonstrate an unwillingness to effectively administer the risk assumed. Responsibilities and accountability may not be clear. Corrective actions are insufficient to address root causes of problems.
Diversification management is effective. Ag concentration limits are set at reasonable levels. Ag concentration risk management practices are sound, including management's efforts to reduce or mitigate exposures. Management effectively identifies and understands correlated risk exposures and their potential effects.	Diversification management is adequate, but certain aspects may need improvement. Ag concentrations are identified and reported, but limits and other action triggers may be absent or moderately high. Concentration management efforts may be focused at the individual loan level, while portfolio-level efforts may be inadequate. Correlated exposures may not be identified and their risks not fully understood.	Diversification management is passive or deficient. Management may not identify concentrations, or take little or no action to reduce, limit, or mitigate the associated risk. Limits may be present but represent a significant portion of capital. Management may not understand exposure correlations and their potential effects. Concentration limits may be exceeded or raised frequently.

Strong	Satisfactory	Weak
Loan management and personnel compensation structures provide appropriate balance between loan/revenue production, loan quality, and portfolio administration, including risk identification.	Loan management and personnel compensation structures provide reasonable balance between loan/revenue production, loan quality, and portfolio administration.	Loan management and personnel compensation structures are skewed to loan/revenue production. There is little evidence of substantive incentives or accountability for loan quality or portfolio administration.
Ag staffing levels and expertise are appropriate for the size and complexity of Ag activities. Staff turnover is low and the transfer of responsibilities is orderly. Training programs facilitate ongoing staff development.	Ag staffing levels and expertise are generally adequate for the size and complexity of the Ag activities. Staff turnover is moderate and may result in some temporary gaps in portfolio management. Training initiatives are adequate.	Ag staffing levels and expertise are deficient. Turnover is high. Management does not provide sufficient resources for staff training.
Ag lending policies effectively establish and communicate portfolio objectives, risk limits as a percentage of total capital, loan underwriting standards, and risk selection standards.	Ag lending policies are fundamentally adequate. Enhancement, while generally not critical, can be achieved in one or more areas. Specificity of risk limits as a percentage of total capital or underwriting standards may need improvement to fully communicate policy requirements.	Ag lending policies are deficient in one or more ways and require significant improvements. Policies may not be clear or are too general to adequately communicate portfolio objectives, risk limits as a percentage of total capital, and underwriting and risk selection standards.
Staff effectively identifies, approves, tracks, and reports significant policy, underwriting, and risk selection exceptions individually and in aggregate, including risk exposures associated with off-balance-sheet activities.	Staff identifies, approves, and reports significant policy, underwriting, and risk selection exceptions on a loan-by-loan basis, including risk exposures associated with off-balance-sheet activities; however, little aggregation or trend analysis is conducted to determine the effect on portfolio quality.	Staff approves significant policy exceptions but does not report them individually or in aggregate or does not analyze the effect of exceptions on portfolio quality. Risk exposures associated with off-balance-sheet activities may not be considered. Policy exceptions may not receive appropriate approval.
Credit analysis is thorough and timely, both at underwriting and periodically thereafter.	Credit analysis appropriately identifies key risks and is conducted within reasonable time frames. Monitoring may need improvement.	Credit analysis is deficient. Analysis is superficial and key risks are overlooked. Credit data are not reviewed in a timely manner.
Risk rating and problem loan review and identification systems are accurate and timely. Credit risk is effectively stratified for both problem and pass-rated credits. Systems serve as effective early warning tools and support risk-based pricing, the ALLL, and capital allocations.	Risk rating and problem loan review and identification systems are adequate. Problem and emerging problem credits are adequately identified, although room for improvement exists. The graduation of pass ratings may need to be expanded to facilitate early warning, risk-based pricing, or capital allocations.	Risk rating and problem loan review and identification systems are deficient. Problem credits may not be identified accurately or in a timely manner, resulting in misstated levels of portfolio risk. The graduation of pass ratings is insufficient to stratify risk in pass credits for early warning or other purposes.

Strong	Satisfactory	Weak
Special mention ratings do not indicate any issues regarding administration of the Ag portfolio.	Special mention ratings generally do not indicate administration issues within the Ag portfolio.	Special mention ratings indicate management is not properly administering the Ag portfolio.
MIS provides accurate, timely, and complete Ag portfolio information. Management and the board receive appropriate reports to analyze and understand the effect of Ag activities on the bank's credit risk profile, including off-balance-sheet activities. MIS facilitates timely exception reporting.	Management and the board generally receive appropriate reports to analyze and understand the effect of Ag activities on the bank's credit risk profile; however, modest improvement may be needed in one or more areas. MIS facilitates generally timely exception reporting.	MIS is deficient. The accuracy or timeliness of information may be affected in a material way. Management and the board may not be receiving sufficient information to analyze and understand the effect of Ag activities on the credit risk profile of the bank. Exception reporting requires improvement.

Appendix C: USDA Guarantee Programs

The USDA has a number of loan guarantee programs intended to assist small farmers and residents of rural communities. The programs described in this section were originally implemented by the FmHA, an agency within the USDA. Although the FmHA was abolished in reorganization, its programs remain intact and are administered by other units within the USDA, such as the FSA.

Farm Service Agency

Farm lending by the FSA is probably the most familiar of the government loan programs in rural areas. FSA guaranteed loans are direct obligations of the U.S. government. The FSA operates numerous offices and administers the USDA's commodity income and price support programs, farm credit programs, marketing programs, and federal crop insurance programs. FSA loans serve as the federal government's primary credit safety net for Ag producers. To qualify for loans, an applicant must demonstrate sufficient farm training or farm experience and be a current or future operator of a family-size (or smaller) farm.

The FSA provides credit assistance to farmers through two mechanisms: loan guarantees and direct loans. Direct loans are made and serviced directly by FSA staff, often at subsidized interest rates and concessionary terms and collateral requirements. The FSA also guarantees certain types of loans made and serviced by qualified commercial or cooperative lenders.

Loan guarantees: Under a guaranteed loan, the FSA guarantees repayment of up to 90 percent of a loan made by a qualifying lender if the borrower defaults. A 95 percent guarantee is available for the refinancing of direct loan program debt or for farmers who qualify for a beginning farmer program.

The FSA can guarantee operating loans (OL) or farm ownership loans (FO) up to an amount that is adjusted annually based on inflation.[4] An FSA guarantee is transferable, and many guaranteed loans are sold through formal and informal secondary markets. While the FSA makes some guaranteed loans directly, commercial banks are the major source of guaranteed loans. Interest rates are negotiated between the lender and the borrower but are not to exceed the average rate the lender offers its farm customers. This requirement and the government's assumption of risk provide borrowers with more favorable rates than the borrower may be able to obtain without a guarantee. Under the Interest Assistance Program, the FSA can provide interest rate subsidies of up to 4 percentage points on guaranteed loans.

Guaranteed loans are the property and responsibility of the lender. The lender makes the loan and services it to conclusion. If successful, the borrower is able to repay the loan and no taxpayer money is used except for administrative expenses. If a loan fails, and the lender suffers a loss, the FSA reimburses the lender with federal funds according to the terms and conditions specified in the guarantee. The lender must notify the FSA when a borrower is

---

[4] Annual adjustments for inflation and updated guarantee maximums can be accessed at www.fsa.usda.gov/FSA. The limit for fiscal year 2014 was $1,355,000.

30 days overdue on a payment and unlikely to bring the account current within 60 days, or if the loan is otherwise a problem. Lenders are encouraged to work with borrowers to resolve problems.

Direct loans: The FSA offers three groups of loan programs:

- **Farm ownership:** FO direct and guaranteed loans are available for the purchase or improvement of farm real estate. Guaranteed loans also are available to help owner-operators restructure their debts using real estate equities. FO loans cannot exceed 40 years. For an FO loan, the producer must also own the farm.
- **Operating loans:** OLs are available for purposes including the purchase of livestock and farm equipment, annual operating expenses, the refinancing of existing indebtedness, and essential family living expenses. OLs can also be used to pay for minor improvements to buildings or, under certain conditions, for costs associated with land and water development. OLs are normally repaid within seven years. For an OL, the producer must be the operator of a family farm after the loan is closed.
- **Emergency loans (EM):** EMs are made directly by the FSA. EMs are available to producers in designated areas where property damage or severe production losses have occurred due to a natural disaster, such as a flood or drought. Loans are made for the actual losses arising from the natural disaster. EMs may be made to repair, restore, or replace damaged farm property and to compensate for loss of income based on reduced production of crops or livestock resulting from the disaster. For EM requests over a designated amount, the applicant must provide to the FSA written confirmation from two commercial lenders that the requested credit could not be obtained.

Credit Program Changes and Restrictions

Changes were made to the EM program to reduce program costs. Stricter eligibility requirements are now applied, and asset valuation procedures have been revised. Changes to the EM program are common, and accordingly, a bank should closely monitor any legislative changes to evaluate how the bank's Ag borrowers may be affected by such changes.

Commodity Credit Corporation

The Commodity Credit Corporation (CCC) is a government-owned and -operated corporation created in 1933 to help stabilize and support farm prices and income and to help maintain balanced supplies and the orderly distribution of Ag commodities. The CCC's operations for the USDA include commodity price support and inventory management programs, donations and sales of government-owned stocks for humanitarian or commercial uses, and foreign market development and export credit guarantee programs. In addition, the CCC provides low-interest loans for grain storage.

Among the many programs administered by the CCC, the export credit guarantee programs and the Commodity Price Support Loan and Purchase Program are of particular interest to banks and examiners.

Export credit guarantee programs: The export guarantee programs are intended to encourage U.S. financial institutions to provide financing where they would be unwilling to extend credit in the absence of the CCC guarantee. Under the Export Credit Guarantee Program (GSM-102), which was instituted in 1980, the CCC guarantees, for a fee, payments due to U.S. exporters under deferred payment sales contracts of up to 36 months. The guarantee provides protection against defaults resulting from both commercial and noncommercial risks. The Intermediate Export Credit Guarantee Program (GSM-103) was implemented in 1986. The program is similar to the GSM-102 program but provides the CCC guarantee to exporters for commodities sold on credit terms in excess of three years, but not more than 10 years. Documentation requirements for the GSM-102 and GSM-103 programs are very specific and require strict adherence to perfect the CCC guarantee.

Commodity Price Support Loan and Purchase Program: Price support is achieved through FSA loans, target price deficiency payments, and purchases of selected commodities at announced levels. Price-supported loans give producers an opportunity to obtain operating cash and remove their crops from the market for potential later sale. Producers are guaranteed at least the support price for the commodity they have pledged as collateral for the loan.

FSA price support loans are nonrecourse loans. If market prices are above support levels, producers may market commodities and pay off loans with interest. If market prices fail to rise above support levels, the producer can deliver the commodity to the CCC and discharge the obligation. When the producer also has operating loans from another lender, the lender is required to sign a lien waiver in favor of the CCC.

Most farm program payments to producers may be assigned to a lender, but price support loans, purchase agreement proceeds, and payments made in the form of commodity certificates are not assignable.

Appendix D: Lending Limits

Generally, national banks and federal savings associations are subject to the same general lending limits (see 12 CFR 32 for both national banks and federal savings associations). There is one additional provision, however, that is applicable only to federal savings associations in the context of Ag lending, as indicated in 12 CFR 32.3(d). This federal savings association exception is described in the lending limits discussion under 12 CFR 32.3 below.

Ag lending is sometimes subject to special lending limits. Summaries of the special lending limits are as follows:

12 CFR 32.3, "Lending Limits"

(a) *Combined general limit.* A bank's total outstanding loans and extensions of credit to one borrower may not exceed 15 percent of the bank's capital and surplus, plus an additional 10 percent of the bank's capital and surplus if the amount that exceeds the bank's 15 percent general limit is fully secured by readily marketable collateral, as defined in 12 CFR 32.2(v). To qualify for the additional 10 percent limit, the bank must perfect a security interest in the collateral under applicable law and the collateral must have a current market value at all times of at least 100 percent of the amount of the loan or extension of credit that exceeds the bank's 15 percent general limit.

(b) *Loans subject to special lending limits.* The following loans or extensions of credit are subject to the lending limits set forth below. When loans and extensions of credit qualify for more than one special lending limit, the special limits are cumulative.

(1) Loans secured by bills of lading or warehouse receipts covering readily marketable staples.

(i) A bank's loans or extensions of credit to one borrower secured by bills of lading, warehouse receipts, or similar documents transferring or securing title to readily marketable staples, as defined in 12 CFR 32.2(w), may not exceed 35 percent of the bank's capital and surplus in addition to the amount allowed under the bank's combined general limit. The market value of the staples securing the loan must at all times equal at least 115 percent of the amount of the outstanding loan that exceeds the bank's combined general limit.

(ii) Staples that qualify for this special limit must be nonperishable, may be refrigerated or frozen, and must be fully covered by insurance if such insurance is customary. Whether a staple is nonperishable must be determined on a case-by-case basis because of differences in handling and storing commodities.

(iii) This special limit applies to a loan or extension of credit arising from a single transaction or secured by the same staples, provided that the duration of the loan or extension of credit is:

(A) Not more than 10 months if secured by nonperishable staples; or

(B) Not more than six months if secured by refrigerated or frozen staples.

(iv) The holder of the warehouse receipts, order bills of lading, documents qualifying as documents of title under the UCC, or other similar documents, must have control and be able to obtain immediate possession of the staple so that the bank is able to sell the underlying staples and promptly transfer title and possession to a purchaser if default should occur on a loan secured by such documents. The existence of a brief notice period or similar procedural requirements under applicable law, for the disposal of the collateral will not affect the eligibility of the instruments for this special limit.

(A) Field warehouse receipts are an acceptable form of collateral when issued by a duly bonded and licensed grain elevator or warehouse having exclusive possession and control of the staples even though the grain elevator or warehouse is maintained on the premises of the owner of the staples.

(B) Warehouse receipts issued by the borrower-owner that is a grain elevator or warehouse company, duly-bonded and licensed and regularly inspected by state or federal authorities, may be considered eligible collateral under this provision only when the receipts are registered with an independent registrar whose consent is required before the staples may be withdrawn from the warehouse.

(3) Loans secured by documents covering livestock.

(i) A bank's loans or extensions of credit to one borrower secured by shipping documents or instruments that transfer or secure title to or give a first lien on livestock may not exceed 10 percent of the bank's capital and surplus in addition to the amount allowed under the bank's combined general limit. The market value of the livestock securing the loan must at all times equal at least 115 percent of the amount of the outstanding loan that exceeds the bank's combined general limit. For purposes of this subsection, the term "livestock" includes dairy and beef cattle, hogs, sheep, goats, horses, mules, poultry, and fish, whether or not held for resale.

(ii) The bank must maintain in its files an inspection and valuation for the livestock pledged that is reasonably current, taking into account the nature and frequency of turnover of the livestock to which the documents relate, but in any case not more than 12 months old.

(iii) Under the laws of certain states, persons furnishing pasturage under a grazing contract may have a lien on the livestock for the amount due for pasturage. If a lien that is based on pasturage furnished by the lienor prior to the bank's loan or extension of credit is assigned to the bank by a recordable instrument and protected against being defeated by some other lien or claim, by payment to a person other than the bank, or otherwise, it will qualify under this exception provided the amount of the perfected lien is at least equal to the amount of the loan and the value of the livestock is at no time less than 115 percent of the portion of the loan or extension of credit that exceeds the bank's combined general limit. When the amount due under the grazing contract is dependent upon future performance, the resulting lien does not meet the requirements of the exception.

(4) *Loans secured by dairy cattle.* A bank's loans and extensions of credit to one borrower that arise from the discount by dealers in dairy cattle of paper given in payment for the cattle may not exceed 10 percent of the bank's capital and surplus in addition to the amount allowed under the bank's combined general limit. To qualify, the paper:

(i) Must carry the full recourse endorsement or unconditional guarantee of the seller; and

(ii) Must be secured by the cattle being sold, pursuant to liens that allow the bank to maintain a perfected security interest in the cattle under applicable law.

(5) (Not related to agriculture)

(c) *Loans not subject to the lending limits.*

(d) *Special lending limits for savings associations.*

(1) $500,000 exception. If a savings association's aggregate lending limitation is less than $500,000, such savings association may have total loans and extension of credit, for any purpose, to one borrower outstanding at one time not to exceed $500,000.

(2) (Not related to agriculture)

(3) (Not related to agriculture)

Appendix E: Glossary

Acre: The unit of measure most typically used to describe land area in the United States. An acre is equivalent to 43,560 square feet and is about nine-tenths the size of a football field.

Agister's lien: A statutory lien granted in most states to help ensure that a feedlot is paid for feed and yardage services rendered. A perfected agister's lien grants the feedlot a first security interest in a customer's cattle and takes preference over a purchase money security interest.

Agribusiness: An enterprise that derives a significant portion of its revenues from sales of agricultural products or sales to agricultural producers.

Agriculture Extension Service: Cooperative (federal, state, and county) agency doing research and education for rural and urban producer and consumer groups, located in each county with specialist personnel for each particular area.

Agronomy: The science of crop production and soil management.

Artificial insemination: Placing semen into the female reproductive tract (usually the cervix or uterus) by means other than natural service. Artificial insemination is commonly used to breed livestock in the dairy, beef, and hog industries.

Average daily gain: Measurement used to calculate the pounds of live weight gained per day.

Backgrounding: Growing program for feeder cattle from the time calves are weaned until they are on a finishing ration in the feedlot.

Barrow: Castrated male pigs raised for meat purposes.

Basis: The difference in price between the Chicago Board of Trade price and a local delivery market price. The basis is typically higher in the northern and western Corn Belt because of the cost of transportation. The basis for any commodity fluctuates during the year and increases or decreases because of supply and demand factors.

Basis contract: A type of forward contracting in which participants lock in a set basis and establish a price for the commodity at a future date.

Beef cattle breeds: Angus, Beefmaster, Belted Galloway, Brahman, Brangus, Charolais, Chianina, Devon, Gelbvieh, Hereford, Limousin, Lincoln Red, Maine Anjou, Murray Grey, Normande, Piedmontese, Red Angus, Salers, Santa Gertrudis, Shorthorn, Simmental, and Texas Longhorn.

Biosecurity: Any of a broad range of practices enforced at a livestock farm to prevent transmittal of pathogens from other sources by feed, livestock, people, or other animals.

Boars: Male hogs used for breeding purposes.

Broiler: Chicken, sometimes called a fryer, reared primarily for meat production. Age to market weight (five to eight pounds) is typically six to eight weeks.

Bt corn: Corn that has received a gene transferred from a naturally occurring soil bacterium called Bacillus Thuringiensis. The gene causes the corn plant to produce one of several insecticidal compounds commonly called Bt toxins. The toxins affect the midgut of particular groups of insects, such as the European corn borer, that can be harmful to corn.

Bulk tank: A refrigerated, stainless steel tank in which milk is cooled quickly to 2 to 4 Celsius (35 to 39 Fahrenheit) and stored until collected by a bulk tank truck for shipping to a milk plant.

Bull: Male bovine, usually of breeding age.

Bunker silo: A horizontal silo, usually eight to 20 feet deep, that holds compacted silage. The sides are normally constructed with concrete panels. A pay loader or similar type of tractor and loader is used to unload this type of storage facility.

Bushel: A unit of dry volume typically used to quantify crop yields. One bushel is equivalent to 32 quarts. The bushel weight of a particular crop varies with the density and bulk of the commodity. For example, oats weigh 32 pounds per bushel (lbs/bu), barley 46 lbs/bu, and corn 56 lbs/bu.

Byproduct: Product of considerably less value than the major product. For example, hide and offal are byproducts when beef is slaughtered and processed.

Calf: A male or female bovine under one year of age. Usually referred to as calves until reaching sexual maturity.

Calve: Giving birth to a calf. Same as parturition.

Carryover debt: Any amount of short-term operating debt left unpaid because of the borrower's inability to generate sufficient income to repay the debt. The unpaid amount is typically restructured into a longer-term loan.

Cash grain: Harvested crops to be sold in the market.

Center pivot: A type of irrigation system that consists of a wheel-driven frame that supports a series of sprinkler nozzles. The frame rotates about a central point to distribute water over a large circular area.

Cereal grains: Plants of the grass family that produce grain (seeds) for human food. They include wheat, rice, barley, oats, corn, rye, and triticale.

Chattel property: Loan collateral other than real estate used by borrowers to secure a loan. Examples include farm machinery and equipment, livestock, stored grain, and growing crops.

Commodity Credit Corporation (CCC): A lending arm of the USDA participating as a lender in the FSA's farm loan programs when farmers "seal" their grain and obtain CCC loans at below market interest. In addition, the CCC provides low-interest loans for grain storage.

Confinement: A development process where livestock are kept in dry-lot for maximum, year-round production. Facilities may be floored, enclosed, or covered partially or completely.

Conservation plan: Cropping plan developed to minimize soil erosion on highly erodible land. Conservation plans must be developed and followed to qualify for various FSA programs.

Conservation Reserve Program: A federal program under which producers voluntarily retire environmentally sensitive cropland for 10 to 15 years in return for annual rental payments. The USDA shares the cost of establishing approved conservation practices. Payments are made through the CCC.

Conservation tillage: Any tillage and planting system that covers 30 percent or more of a planted soil surface with crop residue to reduce soil erosion.

Contracting production: A contract agreement that allows a farmer to sell crops at a predetermined price at a specified date as stated in the contract.

Conventional tillage: Tillage used to cultivate the entire soil surface and performed before planting.

Cooperative: An organization formed for the production and marketing of goods or products owned collectively by members, who share in the benefits. The most common examples in agriculture involve dairy processing plants, grain elevators, and crop input suppliers.

Corn Belt: The area of the United States where corn is a principal cash crop, including Iowa, Indiana, most of Illinois, and parts of Kansas, Missouri, Nebraska, South Dakota, Minnesota, Ohio, and Wisconsin.

Cover crop: Crop planted to improve soil or prevent erosion.

Cow: A mature female bovine. Usually referring to any female that has calved.

Cow/calf operation: Cattle operation owning beef cows with income derived from the successful reproduction and sale of feeder calves.

Crop hail insurance: Insurance against hail damage, typically based on a dollar value coverage per acre.

Crop share lease: Land leased by a farmer in exchange for a percentage of the crop.

Cull: Animals no longer desired for production or breeding purposes and sold for slaughter.

Custom operator: Contracted machine operator who does custom work on an hourly or acreage basis.

Custom work: Machine work, particularly crop planting or harvesting, done for others on an hourly or acreage basis.

Cwt.: Abbreviation for hundredweight, a common measure for raw agricultural products. Sales of hogs, cows, and milk are priced by the hundredweight, or cwt.

Dairy cattle breeds: Ayrshire, Brown Swiss, Guernsey, Holstein-Friesian, and Jersey.

Dairy cow: A female bovine that has calved and is producing milk for human consumption.

Dairy steer: A castrated male of any of the dairy cattle breeds, raised for meat production.

Disaster payments: Financial aid paid to farmers and livestock producers who suffer heavy economic losses from natural disasters such as flooding, damaging wind, and drought. Usually refers to federal funds administered through the USDA.

Dry cow: A cow that has completed its lactation period and is no longer producing milk. The dry period is used to prepare the cow for calving and the next lactation cycle.

Dryland farming: The practice of crop production without irrigation.

Dry lot: An open lot, sometimes covered with concrete, that has no vegetative cover. Generally used as exercise areas in most of United States but may be used as primary cattle housing in the more arid climates.

Erosion: The wearing away of the land surface, usually by running water or wind.

Ewe: A mature female sheep.

Farm Credit Administration (FCA): An independent agency of the Executive Branch of the federal government of the United States. It was created by a 1933 Executive Order of President Franklin D. Roosevelt and derives its authority from the Farm Credit Act of 1971, as amended. The mission of FCA is to ensure a safe, sound, and dependable source of credit and related services for agriculture and rural America.

Farm Credit System (FCS): A nationwide network of borrower-owned lending institutions providing financing and services to agricultural and rural borrowers. The FCS is a government-sponsored entity and obtains funding from the Federal Farm Credit Banks Funding Corporation through bond sales.

Farm Service Agency (FSA): Formerly known as Farmers Home Administration. The FSA administers federal agricultural lending and policy programs.

Farrowing: The birthing process for pigs.

Farrowing house: Facility for birthing and nursing piglets.

Farrow to finish operation: A hog production system containing all production phases: breeding, gestation, farrowing, nursery, grow-finishing, and market.

Fed cattle: Cattle that have been finished and sold in the market for meat consumption (average weight 1,200 to 1,400 pounds).

Feed: Any grain, hay, or forage used as animal feed.

Feeder livestock: Animals, such as cattle or pigs, that are raised to an optimum market weight for slaughter purposes.

Feeder pig operation: The operator farrows sows, raises the piglets through the nursery phase, and sells the pigs to a finishing operation to grow them out to market weight.

Feed grains: Grain grown for feeding to animals. Examples include corn, sorghum, and most barley; barley also is grown for malting purposes, however, in which case it is classified as a small grain.

Feedlot: Enterprise in which cattle are fed grain and other concentrates, usually for 90 to 120 days. Feedlots can range in capacity from fewer than 100 head to many thousands.

Finishing house: Facility for feeding and raising pigs until they attain market weight, usually 225 to 250 pounds.

Forage: Feedstuffs composed primarily of the whole plant, including stems and leaves.

Forage crop: Annual or perennial crops grown primarily to provide feed for cattle. During harvesting operations, most of the aboveground portion of the plant is removed from the field and processed for later feeding.

Forward contract: A form of marketing in which specific bushels of grain, pounds of milk, or pounds of beef or hogs are sold at a set price at a future date.

Free stalls: Resting cubicles, or "beds," in which dairy cows are free to enter and leave, as opposed to being confined in stanchions or pens.

Fresh cow: A cow that has recently given birth.

Futures contract: A marketing mechanism in which farm commodities are bought and sold in established quantities. If a futures position is not canceled, the buyer or seller of the contract must either take or make delivery of the contracted commodity.

Genetically modified organism (GMO): A term that refers to plants with genes implanted to improve their performance by making them resistant to certain pesticides, diseases, or insects.

Gestation period: The amount of time between conception and delivery of newborn livestock.

Gilts: Young female hogs used for farrowing pigs or finished for slaughtering.

Grade A dairy: A dairy producing milk for human drinking purposes under state-approved sanitation conditions. Milking barn and milk-handling equipment must meet certain state regulations.

Grade B dairy: A dairy producing milk for making cheese, ice cream, or condensed or powdered milk. Sanitation requirements are not as strict as for Grade A production. The milk cannot be sold for fresh market consumption.

Hay: Dried feed consisting of entire plants that can be used as feed for cattle and sheep. Alfalfa, clover, grass, and oats are types of plants dried for hay.

Hedge: Practice of locking in a commodity price by counterbalancing one future transaction against another.

Heifer: Young female bovine that has not calved.

Hog: Generic term, usually applied to growing swine.

Hypothecation agreement: An agreement to pledge collateral on a loan without the lender taking possession of the property.

Lactation: Period of milk production. Typically, a dairy cow produces milk 305 or more days during the year.

Lamb: A young male or female sheep, usually less than one year old. Also a term to describe meat from a sheep less than one year old.

Land contract: A legal contract to deliver a property deed to a purchaser when payments are to be made over a period of time. The purchaser in this type of sale customarily pays a small portion of the purchase price when the contract is signed and agrees to pay additional sums at specific intervals and in specified amounts until the total purchase price is paid. Ownership of the land does not become final until all payments have been made.

Litter: Pigs that are born to a sow at one time, normally eight to 12 piglets.

Loose housing: Facilities allowing cattle access to a large, open bedded area for resting (also known as free housing).

Multi-peril crop insurance: Commonly known as federal crop insurance. Insurance against damage caused by wind, drought, flood, etc. Coverage based on up to 85 percent of established yield. Seventy to 80 percent coverage is the most common.

No-till: A crop production system in which seed is planted in soil that is left undisturbed following harvest. No-till is a farming practice for conserving soil.

Nursery: Facility for housing and raising weaned piglets.

Options contract: A contract providing the participant the right to buy or sell a commodity at a future date.

Out of trust sale: A circumstance where collateral is sold, generally by the borrower to a third party, despite an encumbrance.

Parlor: A specialized area for milking cows on a dairy farm. Parlors come in many types, including flat barn, walk-through, herringbone, parallel, swing, and rotary.

Pasture (or pastureland): Land used primarily for producing domesticated forage plants for livestock (in contrast to rangeland, where vegetation is naturally occurring and is dominated by grasses and perhaps shrubs).

Patronage: A portion of net earnings distributed periodically to each member or patron of a cooperative organization, based on quantity or value of business done with or for the patron.

Pesticide: A general name for agricultural chemicals that include

- herbicides, for the control of weeds and other plants.
- insecticides, for the control of insects.
- fungicides, for the control of fungi.
- nematocides, for the control of parasitic worms.
- rodenticides, for the control of rodents.

Pig: Term usually applied to young, immature swine.

Piglet: Baby pig weighing up to 20 to 25 pounds.

Pipeline: A stainless steel or glass pipe used for transporting milk.

Pit: A contained structure with concrete walls in which liquid or semiliquid manure is stored.

Poult: Young turkey chick.

Precision farming: A farm management concept based on observing and responding to intra-field variations. Precision farming relies on Global Positioning System (GPS) technology to tailor soil and crop management to fit the specific conditions within a field or tract of land.

Pre-selling production: Contracting for the sale of crops or livestock before they are ready for market.

Pullet: Young female chicken from day of hatching through onset of egg production.

Replacement heifers: Heifers raised to replace the dairy or beef cows producing in the herd. An open heifer is typically less than 15 months old and is not pregnant. A bred heifer is pregnant with its first calf. A springing heifer is bred and within a month of calving.

Roughage: Feed that is high in fiber, low in digestible nutrients, and low in energy (e.g., hay, straw, silage, and pasture).

Self-propelled: Farm machines with integral power units capable of moving about, as well as performing some other simultaneous operation such as harvesting or spraying a crop.

Sheep breeds: Charollais, Cheviot, Columbia, Devon, Dorset, Hampshire, Lincoln, Merino, Rambouillet, Southdown, Shropshire, and Suffolk.

Silage: A feed prepared by chopping green forage (e.g., grass, legumes, or field corn) and placing the material in a structure or container designed to exclude air. The material then ferments, retarding spoilage.

Silage bags: Large plastic tubes in which forages are fermented. Plastic is removed and discarded as the ensiled feed is fed.

Silo: A storage facility for silage. Usually referring to upright concrete or fiberglass silos.

Small grain: Barley, oats, rye, triticale, and wheat.

Sold out of trust: A circumstance where a borrower sells property that has been pledged as collateral for a loan to a third party without notifying the lender.

Sows: Female hogs used for producing piglets. Sows have farrowed at least one litter of pigs.

Stanchion barn: A type of dairy barn where animals are housed in individual stalls as opposed to free stalls, where the cattle are free to roam in a confined area.

Steer: A castrated male bovine. Bull calves not kept for breeding are castrated while still young and raised for beef. Castration makes them easier to handle and produces better-flavored meat.

Stock cows: Female beef cattle used to produce feeder calves. They are also commonly known as range cattle.

Stocker: A weaned feeder calf fed high-roughage diets (including grazing) before going into the feedlot.

Summer fallow: Land cultivated (usually in spring) and left unplanted through the summer.

Swine breeds: American Landrace, American Yorkshire, Berkshire, Chester White, Duroc, Hampshire, and Poland China.

Tenant farmer: Principally operates on rented or leased land.

Tillable acreage: Land suitable for crop production. Total acres less farmstead, waterways, tree lines, and pasture.

Tillage: The mechanical cultivation of soil performed to nurture crops. Tillage can be performed to accomplish a number of tasks, including seedbed preparation, weed control, and crop chemical incorporation.

Topsoil: The layer of soil used for cultivation, which usually contains more organic matter than underlying materials.

Total mixed ration: The blending of various feedstuffs into a single formulated ration, which is fed to cattle on a daily basis. Mixing wagons or stationary mixers are used to blend the various feed ingredients together.

Transgenic crop: Contains a gene or genes that have been artificially inserted instead of the plant acquiring the gene(s) through pollination. The inserted gene(s) may come from an unrelated plant or from a completely different species.

Uniform Commercial Code (UCC): A coordinated code of laws governing the legal aspects of business and financial transactions in the United States. It regulates such topics as the sale of goods, commercial paper, bank deposits and collections, letters of credit, bank transfers, and documents of title. (Note: Not adopted uniformly throughout the United States and not adopted in Louisiana.)

U.S. Department of Agriculture (USDA): Includes the following agencies and units: Foreign Agricultural Service; Food Safety and Inspection Service; Forest Service; National

Resources Conservation Service; Rural Business-Cooperative; Food and Nutrition Service; Center for Nutrition Policy and Promotion; Agricultural Marketing Service; Animal & Plant Health Inspection Service; Grain Inspection, Packers, and Stockyards Administration; Agricultural Research Service; Office of Community Development; Rural Housing Service; Rural Utilities Service; Cooperative State Research Education & Extension Service; Economic Research Service; and National Agricultural Statistics Service.

Value-added products: A general term that refers to agricultural products that have increased in value due to processing. Examples include corn oil and soybean meal.

Veal: A calf (usually male) raised on milk and intended for slaughter at a young age.

Vertical integration: The combining of two or more successive steps in the production, processing, and distributing processes under a single decision-making body. A canner that produces some of its own raw product, a group of farmers that acquires a cannery or cotton gin, or a feed company that owns poultry are all examples of vertical integration.

Warehouse receipt: Document listing goods or commodities kept for safekeeping in storage. Generally represents title to goods or commodities.

References

Laws

7 USC 1631, "Protection for Purchasers of Farm Products"

12 USC 24, "Corporate Powers of Associations" (national banks)

12 USC 84, "Lending Limits" (national banks)

12 USC 371, "Real Estate Loans" (national banks)

12 USC 1464(c), "Loans and Investments" (federal savings associations)

12 USC 1464(u), "Limits on Loans to One Borrower" (federal savings associations)

42 USC 9601 chapter 103, "Comprehensive Environmental Response, Compensation, and Liability Act" (CERCLA)

Regulations

7 CFR 1400-1499, "Loans Relating to Commodity Credit Corporation Programs"

12 CFR 22 (national banks) and 12 CFR 172 (federal savings associations), "Loans in Areas Having Special Flood Hazards"

12 CFR 30, appendix A (II)(C) (national banks), and 12 CFR 170, appendix A (II)(C) (federal savings associations), "Loan Documentation"

12 CFR 32, "Lending Limits" (national banks and federal savings associations)

12 CFR 34, subpart C (national banks), and 12 CFR 164 (federal savings associations), "Appraisals"

12 CFR 34, subpart D (national banks), and 12 CFR 160.101 (federal savings associations), "Real Estate Lending Standards"

12 CFR 160.30, "General Lending and Investment Powers" (federal savings associations)

12 CFR 160.160, "Asset Classification" (federal savings associations)

12 CFR 160.170, "Records for Lending Transactions" (federal savings associations)

13 CFR 121, "Small Business Size Regulations"

Comptroller's Handbook

Examination Process
"Bank Supervision Process"
"Community Bank Supervision"
"Federal Branches and Agencies Supervision"
"Large Bank Supervision"
"Sampling Methodologies"

Safety and Soundness, Asset Quality
"Allowance for Loan and Lease Losses"
"Commercial Real Estate Lending"
"Concentrations of Credit"
"Loan Portfolio Management"
"Rating Credit Risk"

OCC Issuances

OCC Bulletin 2010-42, "Sound Practices for Appraisals and Evaluations: Interagency Appraisal and Evaluation Guidelines" (December 10, 2010)
OCC Bulletin 2013-29, "Third-Party Relationships: Risk Management Guidance" (October 30, 2013)